Misguided Majority: Exposing Flaws in Contemporary Beliefs

Shah Rukh

Published by Shah Rukh, 2024.

While every precaution has been taken in the preparation of this book, the publisher assumes no responsibility for errors or omissions, or for damages resulting from the use of the information contained herein.

MISGUIDED MAJORITY: EXPOSING FLAWS IN CONTEMPORARY BELIEFS

First edition. June 10, 2024.

Copyright © 2024 Shah Rukh.

Written by Shah Rukh.

Table of Contents

Chapter 1: Introduction

The concept of collective wisdom—the idea that a group's decision-making and knowledge aggregation surpass the capabilities of individual members—is deeply ingrained in contemporary societal and organizational paradigms. It's commonly believed that when diverse opinions and knowledge bases come together, the resulting decisions are more accurate and beneficial than those made by individuals. This belief is reflected in practices ranging from democratic governance and crowdsourcing to collaborative work environments and online platforms that rely on user-generated content.

However, the notion of collective wisdom can often be more of an illusion than a reality. This illusion arises from various factors, including cognitive biases, social dynamics, misinformation, and systemic issues within the structures that facilitate group decision-making. By examining these factors in detail, it becomes evident that the presumed superiority of collective judgment is not always guaranteed and can sometimes lead to suboptimal, or even harmful, outcomes.

One significant aspect of the illusion of collective wisdom is the tendency for groups to amplify, rather than mitigate, individual biases. Cognitive biases are systematic errors in thinking that affect decisions and judgments. In group settings, biases such as confirmation bias, where individuals seek out information that confirms their preconceptions, can become even more pronounced. Group members often influence each other, leading to a convergence of opinion that reinforces shared biases. This phenomenon, known as groupthink, results in a lack of critical evaluation and dissenting opinions, ultimately leading to poorer decision-making outcomes.

Another factor contributing to the illusion of collective wisdom is the unequal distribution of influence within groups. Despite the ideal of egalitarian participation, not all voices carry the same weight in group discussions. Factors such as status, confidence, and communication skills can disproportionately elevate certain individuals' opinions over others, irrespective of their actual expertise or the quality of their arguments. This can lead to situations where group decisions are overly swayed by a few dominant members, undermining the supposed benefits of diverse input.

Misinformation and the dissemination of false information further complicate the dynamics of collective wisdom. In an age where information is abundant but not always accurate, the ability to discern truth from falsehood is crucial. However, groups are often susceptible to the spread of misinformation, which can distort collective understanding and decision-making. This is particularly evident in the context of social media, where algorithms prioritize content that generates engagement, often at the expense of accuracy. The viral nature of misinformation on these platforms can lead to widespread misconceptions and reinforce erroneous beliefs within groups.

Moreover, the structure and process of group decision-making can introduce systemic flaws that detract from the quality of collective wisdom. Traditional democratic systems, for instance, rely on the assumption that voters are informed and rational actors. However, numerous studies have shown that voters are often influenced by heuristics, emotional appeals, and superficial factors rather than a deep understanding of policies and issues. This can lead to the election of leaders and the implementation of policies that do not necessarily reflect the collective best interest. Similarly, in corporate environments, hierarchical structures can impede the flow of information and stifle innovative ideas from lower-level employees, thereby limiting the potential for true collective wisdom.

The illusion of collective wisdom is also perpetuated by the myth of the "wisdom of the crowd," which suggests that aggregating the opinions of a large number of people leads to superior decisions. While there are situations where crowds can indeed make accurate judgments—such as guessing the weight of an object when the median of individual estimates is taken—this is not universally applicable. The effectiveness of crowd wisdom relies on conditions such as diversity of opinion, independence of judgments, and decentralized decision-making. In practice, these conditions are often not met. Group members may not have access to independent information, may be influenced by each other's opinions, and may be subject to centralizing forces that skew the aggregation process. As a result, the decisions made by crowds can be as flawed as those made by individuals or small, unrepresentative groups.

Furthermore, the reliance on collective wisdom can lead to the abdication of individual responsibility. When individuals believe that a group's decision will inherently be better or more accurate, they may be less inclined to critically evaluate information or advocate for their own viewpoints. This phenomenon can lead to a diffusion of responsibility, where no one feels accountable for the group's decisions, ultimately resulting in poorer outcomes. In extreme cases, this can manifest in situations where harmful or unethical decisions are made because individuals within the group assume that collective decision-making processes will correct any issues.

The illusion of collective wisdom is not only a matter of flawed decision-making processes but also a reflection of broader societal dynamics. It underscores the challenges of achieving true inclusivity and equity in group settings. Despite the ideal of diverse participation, social, economic, and political inequalities often limit the extent to which all voices are heard and valued. This is evident in various contexts, from community meetings where marginalized groups may lack the confidence or resources to participate fully, to corporate boardrooms where decision-making power is concentrated among a homogeneous group of elites. The belief in collective wisdom can obscure these power imbalances and perpetuate systemic inequities, leading to decisions that favor the interests of the dominant group rather than reflecting the needs and perspectives of the wider community.

Addressing the illusion of collective wisdom requires a critical examination of the structures and processes that underpin group decision-making. It necessitates a commitment to fostering genuine inclusivity, ensuring that diverse perspectives are not only represented but actively listened to and incorporated into decision-making. This involves creating environments where dissenting opinions are valued, critical thinking is encouraged, and the potential for biases and misinformation is acknowledged and mitigated. It also calls for a reevaluation of the mechanisms through which collective decisions are made, from electoral systems that better reflect the will of the people to organizational practices that prioritize transparent and equitable decision-making.

Chapter 2: The Echo Chamber Effect

The Echo Chamber Effect is a pervasive phenomenon in today's digital age, largely driven by social media platforms, where individuals find themselves surrounded by information that reinforces their existing beliefs and opinions. This effect has significant implications for the way opinions are formed, spread, and solidified in society, ultimately affecting everything from personal relationships to political landscapes. Understanding the mechanics of the Echo Chamber Effect, its origins, and its impact on social dynamics requires a deep dive into the intricacies of social media's role in shaping opinions.

At its core, the Echo Chamber Effect occurs when individuals interact predominantly with like-minded people and sources of information, leading to a homogeneous information environment. Social media platforms, designed to maximize user engagement and satisfaction, often contribute to this phenomenon by using algorithms that prioritize content aligning with users' pre-existing preferences and interests. These algorithms analyze user behavior—such as likes, shares, and search histories—to create personalized feeds that reinforce users' existing viewpoints. This personalization creates a feedback loop where users are continually exposed to similar perspectives, which limits their exposure to diverse viewpoints and fosters a sense of consensus, even if it is illusory.

The origins of the Echo Chamber Effect can be traced back to basic human psychology. Humans have an inherent tendency to seek out information that confirms their beliefs and to avoid information that challenges them, a behavior known as confirmation bias. This bias is magnified in the context of social media, where the sheer volume of information and the speed at which it is disseminated make it easier for individuals to curate their informational environments. Unlike traditional media, which typically offers a broader range of perspectives, social media allows for a high degree of selective exposure, where individuals can follow, like, or subscribe to specific sources that align with their views, further reinforcing their beliefs and insulating them from opposing opinions.

The structural design of social media platforms exacerbates the Echo Chamber Effect. Platforms such as Facebook, Twitter, and YouTube employ complex algorithms that tailor content to individual users' tastes and preferences. These algorithms are designed to keep users engaged by showing them content that they are likely to agree with or find interesting. The more users engage with particular types of content, the more the algorithm feeds them similar content, creating a self-reinforcing cycle. This tailored content delivery system not only keeps users within their comfort zones but also amplifies their existing views, making them less likely to encounter or consider alternative perspectives.

In addition to algorithmic filtering, the social nature of these platforms plays a critical role in the formation of echo chambers. On social media, users tend to form networks and communities based on shared interests and ideologies. These online communities often become echo chambers where members echo and reinforce each other's views. The social validation that comes from receiving likes, shares, and positive comments from like-minded peers can strengthen individuals' beliefs and make them more resistant to opposing viewpoints. The desire for social acceptance and the fear of conflict or rejection can also lead to self-censorship, where individuals avoid expressing dissenting opinions, further entrenching the dominant views within the community.

The Echo Chamber Effect has profound implications for the way opinions are shaped and propagated in society. One of the most significant impacts is the polarization of public discourse. When individuals are repeatedly exposed to information that confirms their beliefs, they become more entrenched in their views, leading to a polarization of opinions. This polarization is evident in various domains, from politics to social issues, where the gap between opposing viewpoints has widened, and compromise has become increasingly difficult. Polarization can lead to a fragmented society where different groups are not only divided by their beliefs but also by their perceptions of reality.

The impact of the Echo Chamber Effect extends beyond individual beliefs to influence broader social dynamics. In a polarized environment, it becomes challenging to engage in constructive dialogue or find common ground. Echo chambers can foster an us-versus-them mentality, where opposing groups view each other with suspicion and hostility. This division can lead to a breakdown in social cohesion, making it difficult to address complex societal issues that require collaboration and mutual understanding. The lack of exposure to diverse perspectives also means that individuals are less likely to develop the empathy and understanding necessary to bridge divides and work towards common goals.

The Echo Chamber Effect also has implications for democratic processes. In a healthy democracy, informed citizens engage in reasoned debate and consider multiple perspectives before making decisions. However, the prevalence of echo chambers undermines this ideal by creating a fragmented information landscape where individuals are insulated from opposing viewpoints. This insulation can lead to a distorted understanding of issues and candidates, influencing voting behavior and public opinion in ways that may not reflect the true diversity of perspectives within society. The spread of misinformation and the reinforcement of partisan narratives within echo chambers can further skew the democratic process, making it difficult for citizens to make informed choices.

The role of social media in shaping opinions through echo chambers is also evident in the spread of misinformation and fake news. Echo chambers create fertile ground for the rapid dissemination of false or misleading information, as users are more likely to accept and share content that aligns with their pre-existing beliefs. The lack of exposure to diverse viewpoints means that misinformation is less likely to be challenged or corrected, allowing it to spread unchecked within the echo chamber. This can lead to the entrenchment of false beliefs and the perpetuation of myths and conspiracy theories, which can have serious consequences for public understanding and policy.

The implications of the Echo Chamber Effect extend to personal relationships and social interactions. In a world where individuals increasingly curate their informational environments and surround themselves with like-minded peers, there is a risk of creating social bubbles that exclude diverse perspectives. This can lead to a narrowing of horizons and a reduction in the richness and complexity of social interactions. The reinforcement of homogeneous views within these bubbles can make it difficult for individuals to relate to or understand those with different perspectives, leading to a breakdown in communication and an erosion of social cohesion.

Addressing the Echo Chamber Effect requires a multifaceted approach that involves both individual actions and systemic changes. On an individual level, it is important to recognize the tendency towards confirmation bias and make a conscious effort to seek out diverse perspectives and engage with information that challenges existing beliefs. This can involve following a broader range of news sources, engaging in discussions with people who hold different views, and being open to reconsidering one's opinions in light of new information.

On a systemic level, there is a need for greater transparency and accountability in the way social media platforms operate. This includes the development of algorithms that prioritize diverse and balanced content, rather than simply reinforcing users' existing preferences. Platforms should also take steps to combat the spread of misinformation and ensure that users have access to accurate and reliable information. This can involve measures such as fact-checking, promoting media literacy, and providing users with tools to identify and challenge false information.

Chapter 3: Consumer Culture

Consumer culture, a phenomenon deeply ingrained in contemporary society, represents a paradigm where the acquisition of goods and services forms the core of personal fulfillment, identity, and social status. This pursuit of material happiness has profound implications on individual well-being, social structures, environmental sustainability, and global economies. By exploring the historical origins, psychological underpinnings, societal impacts, and environmental consequences of consumer culture, we can better understand its pervasive influence and the challenges it poses.

Historically, the roots of consumer culture can be traced back to the Industrial Revolution in the 18th and 19th centuries, which marked a significant shift in production processes and economic structures. The advent of mass production and the rise of capitalism transformed societies from agrarian economies, where goods were primarily produced for subsistence, to industrial economies, characterized by the mass production of goods for consumption. This shift was accompanied by an increase in disposable income and the availability of a wide range of consumer goods, leading to the emergence of a culture centered around consumption.

The early 20th century saw the further entrenchment of consumer culture, particularly in Western societies, through the rise of advertising and the advent of credit systems. Advertising played a crucial role in shaping consumer desires and creating new markets by associating products with ideals of happiness, success, and social status. The development of credit systems enabled consumers to purchase goods on credit, further fueling consumption by allowing individuals to buy now and pay later. This period also saw the emergence of department stores and mail-order catalogs, which made a wide range of consumer goods accessible to a broader audience.

The psychological underpinnings of consumer culture are rooted in the human desire for happiness, social status, and identity. Consumer culture capitalizes on these desires by promoting the notion that material possessions are key to personal fulfillment and social recognition. This is evident in the pervasive advertising messages that equate owning the latest products with happiness, success, and self-worth. The act of purchasing and owning goods becomes a means of expressing one's identity and social status, leading to a cycle of consumption where individuals continually seek new products to maintain or enhance their sense of self and social standing.

The concept of material happiness is closely linked to the phenomenon of hedonic adaptation, where individuals quickly return to a baseline level of happiness after experiencing positive or negative events. This means that the initial pleasure derived from acquiring new possessions tends to diminish over time, leading individuals to seek new purchases to recapture that sense of satisfaction. This cycle of temporary happiness followed by a return to baseline creates a continual desire for new goods, driving the relentless pursuit of material happiness that characterizes consumer culture.

Consumer culture also has significant implications for social structures and dynamics. The pursuit of material happiness often leads to the formation of social hierarchies based on consumption patterns, where individuals are judged and valued based on their ability to acquire and display wealth. This is evident in the phenomenon of conspicuous consumption, where individuals purchase and display expensive goods to signal their social status and success. The emphasis on material wealth as a marker of social status can lead to social stratification, where individuals and groups are differentiated based on their consumption capabilities, reinforcing existing social inequalities.

In addition to reinforcing social hierarchies, consumer culture also shapes social interactions and relationships. The emphasis on material possessions as symbols of success and identity can lead to a focus on superficial markers of worth, such as the brands one wears or the car one drives, rather than intrinsic qualities such as character or values. This can result in a society where individuals are valued more for their material possessions than for who they are as people, leading to shallow social interactions and a lack of genuine human connection.

The environmental consequences of consumer culture are profound and far-reaching. The relentless pursuit of material happiness leads to the overconsumption of natural resources and the generation of significant amounts of waste, contributing to environmental degradation and climate change. The production, transportation, and disposal of consumer goods require vast amounts of energy and resources, leading to deforestation, pollution, and the depletion of natural resources. The emphasis on disposable and short-lived products exacerbates the problem, as goods are quickly discarded and replaced with new ones, creating a cycle of waste that is unsustainable in the long term.

The environmental impact of consumer culture is further amplified by the phenomenon of planned obsolescence, where products are designed to have a limited lifespan or to become outdated quickly, encouraging consumers to purchase new items regularly. This practice not only drives continuous consumption but also leads to increased waste and resource depletion, as old products are discarded to make way for new ones. The environmental cost of this cycle of consumption is significant, contributing to global warming, loss of biodiversity, and the pollution of air, water, and soil.

The global economy is deeply intertwined with consumer culture, as economic growth in many countries is driven by consumption. The focus on continuous economic growth leads to a reliance on increasing consumer spending to sustain economic activity and create jobs. This has resulted in a global economic system that prioritizes consumption and material accumulation, often at the expense of social and environmental well-being. The pursuit of economic growth through consumption also creates economic inequalities, as those with greater purchasing power are able to access and enjoy a higher standard of living, while those with less economic power are often left behind.

The impact of consumer culture on individual well-being is complex and multifaceted. While the acquisition of goods can provide temporary pleasure and a sense of achievement, it often fails to deliver long-term happiness and fulfillment. The focus on material possessions as a source of happiness can lead to a cycle of desire and dissatisfaction, where individuals continually seek new purchases to maintain their sense of well-being. This can result in a sense of emptiness and a lack of genuine fulfillment, as material possessions are ultimately unable to provide the deep and lasting happiness that individuals seek.

The emphasis on material wealth and consumption can also lead to negative psychological outcomes, such as anxiety, depression, and a sense of inadequacy. The pressure to continually acquire and display material possessions can create stress and a sense of competition, leading individuals to feel that they are constantly falling short of societal expectations. The focus on external markers of success can also detract from more meaningful sources of happiness, such as relationships, personal growth, and a sense of purpose, leading to a sense of emptiness and dissatisfaction.

Addressing the challenges posed by consumer culture requires a multifaceted approach that involves changes at both the individual and societal levels. On an individual level, it is important to cultivate a sense of contentment and fulfillment that is not dependent on material possessions. This can involve practices such as mindfulness, gratitude, and a focus on intrinsic values such as relationships, personal growth, and a sense of purpose. By shifting the focus away from material accumulation and towards more meaningful sources of happiness, individuals can break free from the cycle of consumption and find a deeper sense of fulfillment.

On a societal level, it is important to promote sustainable consumption practices and to create economic systems that prioritize social and environmental well-being over continuous economic growth. This can involve policies that encourage the production and consumption of sustainable products, such as those that are durable, repairable, and recyclable, as well as measures to reduce waste and promote resource efficiency. It also involves creating economic systems that prioritize the well-being of all members of society, rather than just those with the greatest purchasing power, and that promote equitable access to resources and opportunities.

Chapter 4: Workaholism

Workaholism, the compulsive need to work excessively and continuously, is a deeply embedded aspect of modern culture, particularly in industrialized nations where productivity and success are often equated with personal worth and social status. The phenomenon of workaholism highlights the growing trend of valuing productivity over well-being, a trend that has significant implications for individuals, organizations, and society as a whole. By delving into the historical context, psychological drivers, societal influences, and consequences of workaholism, we can gain a comprehensive understanding of its impact and explore strategies to address its detrimental effects.

The historical roots of workaholism can be traced back to the Industrial Revolution, which marked a significant shift in the nature of work and the organization of society. The move from agrarian economies to industrial economies led to the establishment of a work ethic that emphasized hard work, discipline, and productivity. The Protestant work ethic, which glorified hard work and viewed idleness as morally reprehensible, played a crucial role in shaping attitudes towards work. This cultural shift laid the groundwork for the modern emphasis on work as a primary source of identity and self-worth.

In the 20th century, the rise of capitalism and the increasing emphasis on economic growth and competition further entrenched the value placed on productivity. The emergence of the corporate culture in the post-World War II era, characterized by long working hours and a focus on career advancement, reinforced the idea that success and fulfillment are achieved through hard work and dedication to one's job. The advent of technology and the globalization of markets have only intensified these pressures, making it easier for work to encroach on personal time and blurring the boundaries between work and leisure.

Psychologically, workaholism can be understood as a complex interplay of individual traits and societal pressures. Individuals who exhibit perfectionist tendencies, high levels of ambition, and a strong need for approval are particularly susceptible to workaholism. These individuals often derive their sense of self-worth and identity from their work, leading them to prioritize work over other aspects of life. The constant pursuit of achievement and recognition can create a cycle of excessive work, where the satisfaction of one goal only leads to the setting of new, even more demanding goals.

Workaholism is also driven by societal norms and expectations that valorize productivity and success. In many cultures, particularly in the United States, Japan, and other industrialized nations, there is a strong cultural narrative that equates hard work with virtue and success with moral worth. This narrative is reinforced by the media, which often glorifies the lives of successful entrepreneurs and business leaders who work long hours and achieve great wealth and status. The social pressure to conform to these norms can lead individuals to prioritize work over their health, relationships, and personal well-being.

The influence of organizational culture and workplace dynamics is another critical factor in the development of workaholism. In many organizations, long working hours and high levels of commitment are viewed as indicators of dedication and competence. Employees who work long hours are often rewarded with promotions, raises, and recognition, creating a culture where workaholism is not only accepted but encouraged. The fear of being perceived as lazy or incompetent can lead employees to overwork, even at the expense of their health and well-being.

The consequences of workaholism are far-reaching and impact individuals, organizations, and society in profound ways. On an individual level, workaholism can lead to a range of negative health outcomes, including chronic stress, anxiety, depression, and burnout. The physical toll of excessive work can manifest in various health issues, such as cardiovascular disease, sleep disorders, and weakened immune function. The mental health effects of workaholism are equally significant, leading to decreased well-being, a sense of isolation, and a diminished quality of life.

Workaholism also has a detrimental impact on personal relationships. The excessive focus on work often comes at the expense of time spent with family and friends, leading to strained relationships and social isolation. Workaholics may neglect their personal lives and responsibilities, causing frustration and resentment among loved ones. The lack of work-life balance can result in a breakdown of family cohesion and support, further exacerbating the negative effects of workaholism on individual well-being.

In the workplace, workaholism can have mixed effects on productivity and organizational culture. While workaholics may initially appear to be highly productive, their excessive work habits can lead to diminishing returns over time. The stress and fatigue associated with workaholism can reduce cognitive functioning, impair decision-making, and increase the likelihood of errors and accidents. The negative health effects of workaholism can lead to increased absenteeism, higher healthcare costs, and a greater likelihood of burnout, all of which can negatively impact organizational performance.

Moreover, the presence of workaholics in the workplace can create a culture of overwork that affects all employees. The pressure to conform to long working hours and high levels of commitment can lead to a toxic work environment where employees feel compelled to sacrifice their well-being for the sake of their job. This can result in decreased morale, lower job satisfaction, and higher turnover rates, ultimately undermining the overall effectiveness of the organization.

At a societal level, workaholism reflects and perpetuates broader cultural values that prioritize economic success and material wealth over well-being and quality of life. The emphasis on work and productivity as the primary means of achieving success and status can lead to a devaluation of other important aspects of life, such as relationships, leisure, and personal growth. This can create a society where individuals are valued more for their economic contributions than for their inherent worth as human beings.

The environmental impact of workaholism is also significant. The relentless pursuit of productivity and economic growth often leads to the overuse of natural resources and environmental degradation. The emphasis on continuous production and consumption contributes to pollution, climate change, and the depletion of natural resources, all of which have long-term consequences for the health and sustainability of the planet.

Addressing the issue of workaholism requires a multifaceted approach that involves changes at both the individual and societal levels. On an individual level, it is important to recognize the signs of workaholism and take steps to establish a healthier work-life balance. This can involve setting boundaries between work and personal time, prioritizing self-care and leisure activities, and seeking support from family, friends, and mental health professionals. It is also important to challenge the cultural narratives that equate success with overwork and to recognize the value of rest, relaxation, and personal fulfillment.

On a societal level, there is a need to shift cultural values and norms towards a greater emphasis on well-being and quality of life. This can involve promoting policies and practices that support work-life balance, such as flexible work arrangements, paid family leave, and reasonable working hours. Organizations can play a crucial role in this shift by fostering a culture that values employee well-being and recognizes the importance of rest and recovery. This can involve implementing policies that discourage excessive work, promoting a healthy work environment, and providing support for employees to manage stress and prevent burnout.

Educational institutions can also contribute to addressing workaholism by teaching students about the importance of balance and well-being. This can involve integrating lessons on mental health, stress management, and the value of leisure and personal growth into the curriculum. By fostering a more holistic approach to success and well-being, educational institutions can help to create a new generation of individuals who prioritize their health and quality of life alongside their professional achievements.

Chapter 5: Educational Elitism

Educational elitism is a pervasive issue that has deeply entrenched itself in modern learning systems. At its core, educational elitism refers to the prioritization and preference given to certain institutions, curricula, and individuals based on perceived superiority, often at the expense of equitable access and inclusive practices. This phenomenon manifests in various forms and has significant implications for society, particularly in how it perpetuates inequality and stifles the potential of many individuals.

One of the primary flaws in our learning systems is the hierarchical structure that places undue emphasis on prestigious institutions. Universities and colleges with storied histories and substantial financial endowments often command greater respect and attract more resources. This creates a self-reinforcing cycle where the rich get richer, both in terms of financial assets and intellectual capital. Students from privileged backgrounds are more likely to gain admission to these elite institutions, further entrenching socio-economic disparities. Meanwhile, institutions that serve less affluent populations struggle with inadequate funding, fewer opportunities, and less recognition, despite often working harder to achieve comparable educational outcomes.

Another significant issue is the standardized testing and admissions processes that favor certain demographics. Tests like the SAT, ACT, GRE, and others are often designed in ways that advantage students from wealthier backgrounds who can afford extensive test preparation resources. These exams are intended to be measures of aptitude and readiness but often end up reflecting a student's socio-economic status more accurately than their potential. The emphasis on high-stakes testing also narrows the curriculum, as schools focus on test preparation at the expense of a more holistic education that includes critical thinking, creativity, and emotional intelligence.

Curriculum design itself often reflects educational elitism. Traditional curricula tend to prioritize Western, Eurocentric perspectives, marginalizing other cultural viewpoints and knowledge systems. This not only alienates students from diverse backgrounds but also impoverishes the educational experience for all students by offering a narrow worldview. A truly inclusive curriculum would embrace a plurality of perspectives, enriching students' understanding and appreciation of global cultures and histories.

Teacher quality and distribution further exacerbate educational inequalities. Highly qualified teachers are often drawn to better-resourced schools, leaving underfunded schools with less experienced or less qualified staff. This disparity in teacher quality has a direct impact on student learning outcomes. Moreover, the teaching profession itself is undervalued in many societies, leading to issues with recruitment and retention, particularly in schools that need the most support.

Educational elitism also manifests in the tracking and streaming of students within schools. From an early age, students are often sorted into different tracks based on perceived ability, which frequently correlates with their socio-economic status. These tracks can become self-fulfilling prophecies, where students placed in lower tracks receive less rigorous instruction and fewer opportunities, limiting their future prospects. This system fails to recognize the potential for growth and development in every student, instead pigeonholing them based on early performance.

The digital divide is another critical aspect of educational elitism. In an increasingly digital world, access to technology and the internet is essential for learning. However, students from lower-income families often lack access to reliable devices and high-speed internet, putting them at a significant disadvantage. This gap was starkly highlighted during the COVID-19 pandemic when remote learning became the norm. Students without adequate technology were left behind, exacerbating existing educational inequalities.

Parental involvement and support are crucial to student success, yet educational elitism affects this area as well. Parents from higher socio-economic backgrounds often have more time, resources, and knowledge to support their children's education, from helping with homework to navigating college admissions processes. In contrast, parents from less privileged backgrounds may struggle to provide the same level of support due to work commitments, language barriers, or lack of familiarity with the education system. This disparity further entrenches the advantages of already privileged students.

Extracurricular opportunities are another area where educational elitism is evident. Wealthier schools and families can afford a wide range of extracurricular activities, from sports to arts to academic clubs, which enrich students' educational experiences and enhance college applications. Students from lower-income backgrounds often lack access to such opportunities, limiting their ability to develop diverse skills and interests.

The impact of educational elitism extends beyond individual students to society at large. By perpetuating socio-economic inequalities, it hampers social mobility and contributes to a more divided and unequal society. The talent and potential of many individuals are wasted because they lack access to the same educational opportunities as their more privileged peers. This not only affects their personal outcomes but also deprives society of their potential contributions.

Addressing educational elitism requires a multifaceted approach. Increasing funding for under-resourced schools is a crucial step, ensuring that all students have access to high-quality education regardless of their background. Reforming standardized testing to better measure student potential rather than socio-economic status is also essential. Developing inclusive curricula that reflect a diversity of perspectives can help create a more equitable learning environment.

Improving teacher training and support, particularly in underserved areas, can help ensure that all students receive high-quality instruction. Efforts to bridge the digital divide are also critical, providing all students with the technology and internet access they need to succeed in a digital world. Supporting parental involvement through community programs and resources can help level the playing field for students from diverse backgrounds.

Chapter 6: Health Fads

Health fads, often touted as the latest and greatest paths to wellness, have become increasingly prevalent in modern society. These trends promise quick fixes, miracle cures, and easy ways to achieve optimal health, frequently appealing to the desire for instant results. However, the pursuit of these fads can be misguided and even detrimental, leading to a range of negative consequences.

The phenomenon of health fads is not new; it has historical roots extending back centuries. However, the rise of the internet and social media has significantly amplified their reach and impact. Modern health fads often begin with anecdotal success stories or celebrity endorsements, quickly gaining traction among the public. The rapid dissemination of information online means that these trends can spread like wildfire, often without adequate scientific backing. This proliferation is fueled by a culture that prioritizes convenience and quick fixes, making people susceptible to the allure of immediate results without a thorough understanding of the potential risks.

One of the primary issues with health fads is the lack of scientific evidence supporting their claims. Many of these trends are based on pseudo-science or incomplete research, which can lead to misinformation. For instance, the anti-vaccination movement gained momentum despite overwhelming evidence supporting the safety and efficacy of vaccines. This health fad, fueled by misinformation, has had dire public health consequences, leading to outbreaks of preventable diseases. Similarly, diets like the ketogenic diet or intermittent fasting often promise rapid weight loss and improved health but may not be suitable for everyone. The scientific community has raised concerns about the long-term effects and potential health risks of such restrictive diets.

Health fads also often involve the commercialization of wellness, where products and services are marketed aggressively to consumers.

The wellness industry, worth billions of dollars, capitalizes on people's desire to improve their health. Supplements, detox teas, and fitness gadgets are frequently promoted with lofty promises but often fail to deliver measurable benefits. Detox products, for example, claim to cleanse the body of toxins, yet there is little scientific evidence to support these claims. The human body has efficient detoxification systems, such as the liver and kidneys, which are far more effective than any marketed product.

The psychological impact of health fads cannot be understated. The constant bombardment of messages promising quick fixes can lead to unrealistic expectations and a sense of failure when these fads do not deliver as promised. This can contribute to a cycle of yo-yo dieting and inconsistent health practices, which are detrimental to both physical and mental health. Additionally, the emphasis on certain body ideals promoted by these fads can exacerbate body image issues and lead to disorders such as orthorexia, an unhealthy obsession with eating "pure" foods.

Moreover, the pursuit of health fads can sometimes lead to neglect of proven, evidence-based health practices. For example, people might forego routine medical check-ups or vaccinations in favor of alternative treatments that are not scientifically validated. This can result in missed diagnoses and untreated conditions, posing serious health risks. In extreme cases, individuals have turned to dangerous practices like consuming unregulated supplements or engaging in extreme diets that can cause significant harm. The tragic case of individuals suffering from severe malnutrition or organ failure due to adherence to unbalanced diets underscores the potential dangers of these fads.

The social dynamics surrounding health fads are also worth examining. Peer pressure and the desire to conform to societal trends can drive people to adopt these practices. Social media influencers and celebrities often play a significant role in propagating health fads, wielding considerable influence over their followers. The phenomenon of "fitspiration," for instance, involves influencers sharing their fitness routines and diets, often without the necessary expertise or qualifications. This can lead to the spread of misinformation and unhealthy practices, as followers attempt to emulate their idols without understanding the potential risks.

Furthermore, health fads often exploit vulnerable populations. Individuals struggling with chronic health conditions, obesity, or mental health issues may be particularly susceptible to the allure of quick fixes. The promise of a miracle cure can be especially enticing for those who have not found relief through conventional medical treatments. This vulnerability is exploited by unscrupulous marketers who prioritize profit over the well-being of consumers. For instance, the marketing of certain weight loss supplements or miracle cures for chronic illnesses often targets desperate individuals, leading to financial exploitation and, in some cases, physical harm.

Another critical aspect to consider is the cultural implications of health fads. Many trends are rooted in cultural appropriation, where traditional practices from different cultures are co-opted and commercialized without proper understanding or respect for their origins. Yoga, for example, has been transformed from a spiritual and holistic practice into a commercial fitness trend, often stripped of its cultural and philosophical significance. This not only undermines the integrity of these practices but also contributes to the commodification of culture.

To counter the negative impact of health fads, it is essential to promote health literacy and critical thinking. Educating the public about the importance of evidence-based health practices and encouraging skepticism towards unverified claims can help mitigate the influence of these fads. Healthcare professionals and educators play a crucial role in this regard, providing reliable information and guidance to help individuals make informed decisions about their health.

Regulation and oversight are also vital in curbing the spread of harmful health fads. Governments and regulatory bodies need to enforce stricter guidelines on the marketing and sale of health products and services. This includes ensuring that claims made by these products are substantiated by scientific evidence and that harmful products are removed from the market. Social media platforms and other online spaces should also be held accountable for the spread of misinformation, implementing measures to flag and remove false health claims.

Moreover, fostering a holistic approach to health and wellness can help shift the focus away from quick fixes and towards sustainable, long-term health practices. This involves promoting balanced diets, regular physical activity, mental health care, and preventive medical practices. Encouraging a culture that values overall well-being rather than perfection can help individuals adopt healthier lifestyles that are not driven by the latest fad but by a genuine understanding of their own health needs.

Chapter 7: Digital Addiction

Digital addiction, often characterized by an excessive and compulsive use of digital devices and the internet, has become a prevalent issue in modern society. With the advent of smartphones, social media, and other online platforms, people are constantly connected to the digital world, leading to significant behavioral, psychological, and social consequences. This continuous connectivity has subtly, yet profoundly, altered how individuals interact, work, and live.

One of the primary consequences of digital addiction is the erosion of face-to-face social interactions. People, especially the younger generation, increasingly prefer virtual communication over in-person conversations. This shift has led to a decline in the quality of personal relationships. The nuances of non-verbal communication, such as body language and facial expressions, are lost in text messages and online chats. As a result, people may find it challenging to develop deep, meaningful connections. The ease of digital communication fosters a culture of superficial relationships, where the number of online friends or followers often matters more than the depth of actual friendships.

Furthermore, digital addiction can severely impact mental health. Constant exposure to social media often leads to the comparison of one's life with the curated, seemingly perfect lives of others. This phenomenon, known as "social comparison," can result in feelings of inadequacy, anxiety, and depression. The pressure to maintain an online persona that aligns with societal expectations can be overwhelming, particularly for teenagers and young adults. Moreover, the addictive nature of social media, driven by algorithms designed to keep users engaged, can create a vicious cycle of dependency, where individuals continuously seek validation and gratification through likes, comments, and shares.

The impact of digital addiction extends to physical health as well. Prolonged screen time is associated with a range of health issues, including eye strain, poor posture, and sleep disturbances. The blue light emitted by screens interferes with the body's natural sleep-wake cycle, leading to insomnia and other sleep disorders. Additionally, the sedentary lifestyle encouraged by excessive use of digital devices contributes to obesity, cardiovascular problems, and other chronic health conditions. The lack of physical activity, coupled with unhealthy eating habits often associated with screen time, exacerbates these health risks.

Academic and professional performance also suffers due to digital addiction. Students and employees find it difficult to concentrate on their tasks when they are constantly distracted by notifications and the urge to check their devices. This constant distraction reduces productivity and the ability to engage in deep, focused work. Multitasking, often touted as a beneficial skill in the digital age, actually hampers cognitive performance and leads to lower quality work. The inability to focus for extended periods impairs learning and memory retention, making it difficult for individuals to acquire and apply new knowledge effectively.

In the workplace, digital addiction manifests as a constant need to be connected and responsive, blurring the boundaries between work and personal life. Employees feel pressured to check their emails and respond to work-related messages even outside office hours, leading to burnout and decreased job satisfaction. This culture of overwork, driven by digital connectivity, contributes to stress and reduces overall well-being. The lack of downtime and the inability to disconnect from work hinders creativity and innovation, as employees do not have the mental space to relax and recharge.

Children are particularly vulnerable to the effects of digital addiction. The early exposure to digital devices can interfere with their cognitive and social development. Excessive screen time can delay language acquisition, reduce attention spans, and impair problem-solving skills. Moreover, children who spend more time on digital devices are less likely to engage in physical play, which is crucial for their physical development and overall health. The exposure to inappropriate content and cyberbullying are additional risks that can have long-term psychological effects on young minds.

Digital addiction also has broader societal implications. The constant connectivity fosters a culture of instant gratification, where people expect immediate responses and quick results. This mentality affects patience and the ability to engage in long-term planning and delayed gratification. Moreover, the overwhelming amount of information available online can lead to information overload, making it difficult for individuals to discern credible sources from misinformation. This has significant implications for public discourse and decision-making, as people may base their opinions and actions on inaccurate or biased information.

The economic impact of digital addiction is also noteworthy. Companies invest heavily in technologies designed to capture and retain user attention, often at the expense of user well-being. The business models of many tech companies rely on ad revenue generated by user engagement, creating a financial incentive to design addictive platforms. This focus on maximizing screen time can stifle innovation in other areas, as resources are diverted towards developing features that keep users hooked rather than those that enhance user experience or address societal needs.

Addressing digital addiction requires a multifaceted approach. Education and awareness are crucial in helping individuals understand the risks associated with excessive digital use and encouraging healthier habits. Schools, workplaces, and communities need to promote digital literacy and teach strategies for managing screen time effectively. Parents and caregivers play a vital role in setting boundaries and modeling healthy digital behaviors for children.

Technology companies also have a responsibility to design products that prioritize user well-being. This includes implementing features that encourage breaks, limit screen time, and provide transparency about data usage and algorithmic recommendations. Policymakers can support these efforts by enacting regulations that promote ethical technology design and protect consumers from exploitative practices.

On a personal level, individuals can take proactive steps to mitigate the effects of digital addiction. This includes setting specific times for using digital devices, creating tech-free zones or periods, and engaging in offline activities that promote physical and mental well-being. Mindfulness practices and digital detoxes can help individuals regain control over their screen time and reconnect with the physical world.

Ultimately, addressing digital addiction is not about eliminating digital devices from our lives but about finding a balance that allows us to reap the benefits of technology without compromising our health, relationships, and overall quality of life. It requires a collective effort from individuals, families, communities, businesses, and governments to create a digital environment that supports healthy and meaningful connections.

Chapter 8: Environmental Ignorance

Environmental ignorance, particularly in the form of climate change denial, is a pervasive issue with far-reaching consequences. Despite overwhelming scientific evidence, a significant portion of the global population either doubts the reality of climate change or dismisses its severity. This denial is not merely an academic debate; it has profound implications for policy-making, environmental health, and future generations. Understanding the roots, manifestations, and impacts of climate change denial is crucial for addressing one of the most pressing challenges of our time.

One of the primary drivers of climate change denial is a lack of understanding or awareness about the science behind climate change. Many people have limited knowledge of how greenhouse gases, primarily carbon dioxide and methane, trap heat in the Earth's atmosphere and lead to global warming. This scientific illiteracy can be attributed to gaps in education systems that do not emphasize environmental science or critical thinking skills. Consequently, individuals are more susceptible to misinformation and pseudoscience, which can be propagated through media, social networks, and even political rhetoric.

The role of misinformation cannot be overstated in the context of climate change denial. Fossil fuel companies and other industries with vested interests have historically funded campaigns to cast doubt on climate science. These campaigns employ tactics similar to those used by the tobacco industry, emphasizing uncertainty and downplaying risks to delay regulatory action. Media outlets, particularly those with ideological biases, can perpetuate these narratives by providing platforms for climate change skeptics and framing the issue as a contentious debate rather than a scientific consensus. This creates a false equivalence, where the views of a small minority of scientists are given the same weight as the overwhelming majority of climate experts.

Political ideology also plays a significant role in climate change denial. In many countries, particularly in the United States, climate change has become a highly polarized issue. Conservatives and libertarians are more likely to deny climate change or its human causes, partly because acknowledging it would necessitate government intervention and regulation, which contradicts their ideological beliefs. This politicization of climate science makes it difficult to achieve bipartisan support for necessary climate policies and creates an environment where scientific facts are overshadowed by political agendas.

Economic concerns further fuel climate change denial. Transitioning to a low-carbon economy requires substantial investment in renewable energy, changes in infrastructure, and potential short-term economic disruptions. Industries dependent on fossil fuels, such as coal mining and oil drilling, face significant economic losses if stringent climate policies are implemented. Workers in these industries may also resist change due to fears of job loss and economic insecurity. As a result, there is a powerful economic incentive to deny or downplay the urgency of climate change to protect existing business models and livelihoods.

Psychological factors also contribute to climate change denial. The concept of climate change is abstract and its impacts are often perceived as distant, both geographically and temporally. This cognitive distance makes it difficult for individuals to perceive climate change as an immediate threat. Additionally, the scale of the problem can induce feelings of helplessness and fear, leading to denial as a coping mechanism. It is easier for some individuals to reject the existence or severity of climate change than to confront the daunting challenge it represents.

The consequences of climate change denial are severe and multifaceted. On an environmental level, denial impedes the implementation of policies needed to reduce greenhouse gas emissions and mitigate the effects of climate change. This inaction exacerbates environmental degradation, leading to more frequent and severe weather events, rising sea levels, and loss of biodiversity. The longer action is delayed, the more difficult and costly it becomes to address these impacts.

Socially, climate change denial undermines public trust in science and experts. This erosion of trust extends beyond climate science and can have broader implications for public health and safety, as seen during the COVID-19 pandemic where scientific advice was similarly disregarded by some segments of the population. When scientific consensus is ignored, it becomes challenging to mobilize collective action on issues that require widespread cooperation and adherence to evidence-based guidelines.

Economically, the refusal to address climate change proactively can result in significant costs. Extreme weather events, such as hurricanes, floods, and wildfires, cause billions of dollars in damage annually. These events disrupt communities, destroy infrastructure, and strain public resources. Investing in climate resilience and adaptation measures now can prevent much higher costs in the future. Furthermore, the transition to a green economy presents economic opportunities in the form of new industries and jobs in renewable energy, energy efficiency, and sustainable agriculture. Climate change denial delays these opportunities and maintains dependence on industries that may become obsolete.

On an international level, climate change denial in one country can hinder global efforts to address the issue. Climate change is a global problem that requires coordinated action. When major emitters of greenhouse gases, such as the United States, do not take significant action, it undermines international agreements and efforts to reduce emissions. This lack of leadership can discourage other countries from taking bold steps, leading to a collective failure to meet global climate goals.

Addressing climate change denial requires a multifaceted approach. Education is paramount; individuals need to understand the science of climate change and the evidence supporting it. Schools and universities should integrate comprehensive environmental education into their curricula, emphasizing critical thinking and scientific literacy. Public awareness campaigns can also play a role in disseminating accurate information and countering misinformation.

Media outlets have a responsibility to report on climate change accurately and responsibly. This includes avoiding false balance in coverage, where fringe views are given undue weight, and highlighting the consensus among scientists. Social media platforms need to address the spread of misinformation by promoting credible sources and fact-checking dubious claims.

Political leaders and policymakers must prioritize climate action and work towards bipartisan solutions. This involves setting aside ideological differences and recognizing the urgent need for collective action. Policies should be informed by scientific evidence and designed to promote economic transition in a just and equitable manner. This includes providing support and retraining for workers in fossil fuel industries and investing in communities that are most vulnerable to the impacts of climate change.

Engaging with local communities is also crucial. Grassroots movements and local initiatives can drive change from the ground up, demonstrating the tangible benefits of sustainable practices. Local governments can implement policies that promote renewable energy, energy efficiency, and sustainable land use, serving as models for broader national efforts.

On a personal level, individuals can make a difference by reducing their carbon footprint, advocating for climate action, and voting for leaders who prioritize environmental sustainability. Collective action, driven by informed and engaged citizens, can create the political will needed to address climate change effectively.

Chapter 9: The Myth of Meritocracy

The concept of meritocracy, the belief that success and advancement in society are based solely on individual merit and effort, is a pervasive narrative in many cultures, especially in Western societies. This ideal suggests that anyone, regardless of their background, can achieve success through hard work, talent, and determination. However, a critical examination reveals that meritocracy is more myth than reality, obscuring deep-rooted social inequities and perpetuating systemic injustices. Unpacking this myth involves exploring the barriers that undermine true meritocratic ideals, the ways in which privilege operates, and the societal implications of adhering to this flawed narrative.

One of the fundamental problems with the concept of meritocracy is that it assumes a level playing field where everyone has equal opportunities to succeed. In reality, numerous structural inequalities create significant disparities in access to resources and opportunities. Socioeconomic status, race, gender, and geographical location are just a few factors that influence an individual's ability to succeed. For instance, children born into wealthier families have access to better educational resources, healthcare, and social networks, all of which provide a substantial head start. In contrast, those from disadvantaged backgrounds often face a multitude of obstacles that hinder their ability to compete on an equal footing.

Education, often touted as the great equalizer in a meritocratic society, actually highlights the fallacies of meritocracy. Quality education is not uniformly accessible; schools in affluent areas typically have better funding, more experienced teachers, and superior facilities compared to those in underprivileged neighborhoods. This disparity begins early in life and compounds over time, making it increasingly difficult for students from lower socioeconomic backgrounds to catch up. Standardized testing, used as a measure of merit, often reflects these inequalities rather than true intellectual ability or potential. As a result, educational attainment and, subsequently, career opportunities are heavily influenced by socioeconomic status rather than pure merit.

The workplace, another arena where meritocracy is purported to prevail, similarly reveals significant inequities. While the narrative suggests that talent and effort are the primary drivers of career advancement, numerous studies have shown that factors such as gender, race, and social connections play a substantial role. Women and minorities often face implicit biases that affect hiring, promotion, and compensation. The glass ceiling and pay gaps are persistent issues, indicating that merit alone does not determine professional success. Networking and social capital, which are more accessible to individuals from privileged backgrounds, also heavily influence career trajectories. These factors collectively undermine the idea that the workplace is a pure meritocracy.

Moreover, the myth of meritocracy serves to justify and perpetuate social inequalities. By promoting the idea that success is solely a result of individual effort, it places blame on those who do not succeed, suggesting that their lack of achievement is due to personal failings rather than structural disadvantages. This narrative absolves society from addressing systemic issues such as poverty, discrimination, and unequal access to education and healthcare. It also creates a sense of complacency among the privileged, who may believe that their success is entirely self-made and therefore do not recognize the advantages they have benefited from.

The concept of meritocracy also overlooks the importance of luck and external circumstances in achieving success. Factors such as the timing of entering the job market, economic conditions, and even health can significantly impact an individual's career path. For example, graduating during an economic recession can limit job opportunities, while entering the job market during a boom can provide a plethora of choices. These elements of chance are rarely acknowledged in discussions about merit, further perpetuating the myth that success is purely the result of individual effort.

Another critical aspect of the meritocracy myth is its psychological impact. The belief in a meritocratic society can lead to increased stress and pressure to succeed, as individuals internalize the idea that their worth is tied to their achievements. This can result in a relentless pursuit of success and a fear of failure, with significant mental health implications. Additionally, those who do not achieve societal standards of success may experience feelings of inadequacy and low self-esteem, believing that their lack of success is due to personal shortcomings rather than external factors beyond their control.

The meritocracy myth also affects public policy and societal attitudes towards welfare and social support systems. If success is viewed as a result of individual effort, then poverty and unemployment are often seen as a consequence of laziness or lack of initiative. This perspective can lead to reduced support for social safety nets and policies aimed at reducing inequality, as there is a belief that individuals should be able to lift themselves out of poverty through hard work alone. This ignores the structural barriers that prevent many people from achieving economic stability and exacerbates social inequalities.

Addressing the myth of meritocracy requires a multifaceted approach. Education systems need to be reformed to ensure more equitable access to quality education, regardless of socioeconomic background. This includes increased funding for schools in disadvantaged areas, early childhood education programs, and initiatives to address implicit biases in standardized testing and admissions processes. Higher education institutions also need to be more accessible, with policies that support students from diverse backgrounds and provide the necessary resources for their success.

In the workplace, promoting diversity and inclusion is essential to counteract the biases that undermine meritocracy. This involves implementing fair hiring practices, providing mentorship and career development opportunities for underrepresented groups, and creating an organizational culture that values and supports diversity. Companies should also recognize the importance of social capital and work to provide networking opportunities for all employees, regardless of their background.

Public policies need to address the structural inequalities that hinder true meritocratic ideals. This includes measures to reduce poverty, improve access to healthcare, and ensure affordable housing. Social safety nets should be strengthened to provide support for those facing economic hardships, recognizing that systemic factors often contribute to these challenges. Additionally, tax policies should be designed to reduce income inequality and provide greater opportunities for social mobility.

On an individual level, it is important to challenge the assumptions underlying the meritocracy myth and recognize the role of privilege and structural factors in success. This involves acknowledging the advantages one may have benefited from and using that awareness to advocate for more equitable policies and practices. It also means supporting initiatives and organizations that work towards social justice and equity, and engaging in conversations that raise awareness about the realities of social inequalities.

Chapter 10: Political Polarization

Political polarization, the increasing ideological distance and hostility between different political factions, has become a defining feature of contemporary democracies. This growing divide is not merely a matter of differing opinions but reflects deep-seated divisions that weaken democratic institutions, erode social cohesion, and undermine the ability to address critical societal challenges. Understanding the roots, manifestations, and consequences of political polarization is crucial for fostering a healthier democratic process and mitigating its adverse effects.

The origins of political polarization are multifaceted, involving a combination of social, economic, and technological factors. One significant driver is the changing media landscape. Traditional media, with its commitment to balanced reporting and journalistic standards, has given way to a more fragmented and partisan media environment. The rise of 24-hour news channels, social media platforms, and online news sources has created echo chambers where individuals are exposed primarily to viewpoints that reinforce their preexisting beliefs. Algorithms designed to maximize user engagement further exacerbate this by curating content that aligns with users' preferences, leading to a narrowing of perspectives and increased ideological rigidity.

Economic inequality also plays a critical role in political polarization. As the gap between the rich and poor widens, different segments of society experience vastly different realities. Economic hardships and perceived injustices can lead to feelings of disenfranchisement and resentment, which are often channeled into political support for more extreme positions. This economic divide fosters a sense of "us versus them," where the interests of different economic classes are seen as fundamentally opposed, further entrenching political divisions.

Demographic changes, particularly in multicultural societies, contribute to polarization as well. The increasing diversity in many countries can lead to tensions over cultural identity, immigration, and social integration. Political parties often exploit these tensions, framing issues in ways that appeal to their base but deepen societal rifts. This is evident in debates over immigration policy, affirmative action, and national identity, which often become highly polarized and emotionally charged.

The political system itself can incentivize polarization. Electoral systems that favor a two-party structure, such as the first-past-the-post system, tend to polarize politics by pushing parties to adopt more extreme positions to differentiate themselves and mobilize their base. Gerrymandering, the practice of redrawing electoral districts to benefit a particular party, also exacerbates polarization by creating "safe" districts where candidates are more likely to face primary challenges from the extremes of their party rather than competitive general elections. This encourages politicians to cater to the more radical elements of their base rather than seeking compromise and consensus.

Polarization manifests in various ways, affecting both political elites and the general populace. Among political leaders, polarization is evident in increased partisanship and a decline in bipartisan cooperation. Legislative bodies become gridlocked as compromise becomes politically costly, leading to stalemates and ineffective governance. Policies are more likely to be passed through narrow partisan majorities, undermining their legitimacy and stability as subsequent administrations seek to overturn them. This legislative dysfunction erodes public trust in government and its ability to address pressing issues.

At the societal level, polarization affects how individuals interact with each other. Political affiliation becomes a significant factor in social identity, influencing personal relationships and social networks. Friendships and even family relationships can become strained or fractured along political lines, leading to social isolation and fragmentation. This social divide is particularly pronounced on social media, where political discourse often devolves into vitriol and hostility. The anonymity and distance provided by online platforms embolden individuals to express extreme views and engage in behavior they might avoid in face-to-face interactions.

The consequences of political polarization are profound and far-reaching. One of the most immediate effects is the erosion of democratic norms and institutions. Democracies rely on a degree of mutual respect and a willingness to accept the legitimacy of political opponents. As polarization intensifies, this mutual respect deteriorates, and opponents are increasingly viewed as existential threats rather than legitimate participants in the democratic process. This delegitimization can lead to efforts to undermine democratic institutions, such as attempts to suppress voting, manipulate electoral outcomes, or weaken checks and balances.

Polarization also hampers effective governance and policy-making. In highly polarized environments, reaching consensus on important issues becomes exceedingly difficult. This leads to policy paralysis, where critical issues such as healthcare, climate change, and economic inequality remain unaddressed. The inability to enact comprehensive and stable policies undermines public confidence in the government and its institutions, contributing to a cycle of disillusionment and disengagement from the democratic process.

Moreover, polarization can exacerbate social and economic inequalities. Policies that favor one political faction often neglect or disadvantage the other, leading to uneven resource distribution and social benefits. This reinforces the grievances of marginalized groups and perpetuates a sense of injustice and alienation. For example, economic policies that favor deregulation and tax cuts for the wealthy can deepen income inequality and reduce social mobility, fueling further political and social polarization.

The international implications of political polarization are also significant. A polarized nation can struggle to present a unified front in foreign policy, weakening its position on the global stage. Internal divisions can be exploited by adversaries, undermining national security and diplomatic efforts. Furthermore, the spread of polarization and populist movements across borders can destabilize international alliances and cooperation, as countries become more inward-focused and less willing to engage in multilateral initiatives.

Addressing political polarization requires a multifaceted approach that tackles both its causes and manifestations. Reforming the media landscape is crucial. This involves promoting media literacy to help individuals critically evaluate information sources and reduce the influence of misinformation and partisan bias. Supporting independent journalism and encouraging platforms to adopt more transparent and balanced algorithms can also help create a more informed and less polarized public discourse.

Electoral and political reforms are essential to mitigate polarization. Implementing measures such as ranked-choice voting or proportional representation can encourage a more diverse range of political voices and reduce the winner-takes-all dynamics that drive polarization. Redistricting reforms to combat gerrymandering can create more competitive electoral districts, incentivizing politicians to appeal to a broader range of voters. Encouraging cross-party dialogue and cooperation, both within legislative bodies and at the community level, can help rebuild trust and promote a culture of compromise.

Economic policies that address inequality and promote social mobility are also vital. Ensuring access to quality education, healthcare, and employment opportunities can reduce the economic disparities that fuel polarization. Policies that support marginalized communities and address systemic injustices can help bridge divides and foster a more inclusive society. This requires a commitment to social justice and equity in policy-making, recognizing the interconnectedness of economic and social inequalities.

On a societal level, fostering a culture of empathy and understanding is crucial. Encouraging dialogue across political divides, promoting civic engagement, and supporting initiatives that bring diverse communities together can help reduce polarization. Education systems should emphasize critical thinking, civic responsibility, and the importance of democratic values. Public leaders and influencers have a role in modeling respectful discourse and highlighting common ground, rather than exploiting divisions for political gain.

Ultimately, overcoming political polarization is about renewing a commitment to the democratic principles of pluralism, mutual respect, and the common good. It requires recognizing the complexity of societal issues and the need for collaborative solutions that transcend partisan lines. By addressing the underlying causes of polarization and promoting a more inclusive and equitable society, we can strengthen the foundations of democracy and build a more resilient and cohesive political community.

This effort is a long-term endeavor that demands sustained engagement from all sectors of society. Governments, civil society organizations, educational institutions, and individuals must all play their part in fostering a more constructive and less polarized political environment. Through collective action and a shared commitment to democratic values, it is possible to bridge divides, restore trust, and ensure that democracy remains robust and responsive to the needs of all citizens.

Chapter 11: Beauty Standards

Beauty standards have been an intrinsic part of human societies throughout history, evolving over time and across cultures. These standards dictate what is considered attractive and desirable, often influencing individuals' self-esteem, behavior, and social standing. In contemporary society, the pursuit of these beauty ideals has become increasingly intense, pervasive, and commercialized, driven by a variety of factors including media, advertising, and social networks. This relentless quest for perfection can have significant psychological, physical, and social consequences, revealing the deeply harmful effects of rigid beauty standards.

At the core of the issue is the definition of beauty itself, which is often narrow and exclusionary. Modern beauty standards, especially in Western cultures, tend to emphasize characteristics such as thinness, fair skin, youth, and specific facial features like high cheekbones and full lips. These ideals are not only unrealistic for the vast majority of people but also reflect a limited and often Eurocentric view of beauty that marginalizes other body types, skin tones, and ethnic features. This narrow definition creates a homogenized view of beauty that overlooks the rich diversity of human appearance.

The media plays a pivotal role in shaping and perpetuating these beauty standards. Television, movies, fashion magazines, and advertising consistently showcase idealized images of beauty that are often digitally altered to remove any imperfections. These images create an unattainable standard of perfection that individuals feel pressured to emulate. The rise of social media has intensified this phenomenon, with platforms like Instagram and TikTok inundating users with carefully curated and filtered images. Influencers and celebrities often present an unrealistic portrayal of beauty and lifestyle, further reinforcing the pressure to conform to these standards.

Advertising, particularly in the beauty and fashion industries, capitalizes on insecurities by promoting products and services that promise to help individuals achieve the ideal look. From skincare and cosmetics to plastic surgery and weight loss programs, the beauty industry is built on the premise that there is always something to fix or improve. This constant barrage of marketing messages can lead to a perpetual cycle of dissatisfaction and consumption, where individuals feel they must continually invest time, money, and effort to meet ever-shifting beauty ideals.

The psychological impact of striving to meet these standards can be profound. For many individuals, particularly women and increasingly men, the pressure to conform to idealized beauty norms can result in feelings of inadequacy, low self-esteem, and body dissatisfaction. This is exacerbated by social comparison, where individuals evaluate their own appearance against the seemingly perfect images they see in the media and on social platforms. This comparison often leads to a distorted self-image and a belief that they fall short of societal expectations.

Body dysmorphic disorder (BDD) is a severe manifestation of the obsession with physical appearance. Individuals with BDD become excessively preoccupied with perceived flaws in their appearance, which are often minor or imagined. This disorder can lead to significant emotional distress, depression, anxiety, and even suicidal thoughts. The prevalence of BDD highlights the extreme consequences of societal pressure to achieve perfection.

Eating disorders are another serious consequence of harmful beauty standards. Disorders such as anorexia nervosa, bulimia nervosa, and binge-eating disorder are often driven by a desire to achieve or maintain a certain body type. These conditions can have devastating effects on physical health, including malnutrition, heart problems, and gastrointestinal issues, and can be fatal if not treated. The link between beauty standards and eating disorders underscores the dangerous lengths to which individuals may go to conform to societal ideals.

The pursuit of beauty through cosmetic procedures is also on the rise, reflecting the normalization of surgical and non-surgical interventions to alter one's appearance. Procedures such as liposuction, breast augmentation, rhinoplasty, and Botox injections have become increasingly common, often fueled by the desire to achieve a specific look promoted by media and celebrity culture. While some individuals find satisfaction and confidence through these procedures, they also carry risks such as surgical complications, infection, and dissatisfaction with the results. Moreover, the normalization of cosmetic surgery can create a vicious cycle where the definition of "natural" beauty becomes increasingly altered, perpetuating unrealistic standards.

The impact of beauty standards is not limited to psychological and physical health; it also has significant social and economic implications. The emphasis on appearance can influence hiring practices, professional advancement, and social interactions. Studies have shown that individuals who conform more closely to societal beauty standards often receive preferential treatment in job interviews, promotions, and salary negotiations. This phenomenon, known as "lookism," discriminates against those who do not meet conventional beauty ideals, limiting their opportunities and perpetuating social inequality.

Children and adolescents are particularly vulnerable to the pressures of beauty standards. From a young age, they are exposed to media images and societal messages that equate physical attractiveness with success and happiness. This early exposure can shape their self-perception and aspirations, leading to body dissatisfaction and unhealthy behaviors. The prevalence of social media among younger generations exacerbates this issue, as platforms that emphasize visual content can amplify feelings of inadequacy and the desire for validation through appearance.

The pressure to conform to beauty standards can also intersect with other forms of discrimination, such as racism, sexism, and ageism. For instance, beauty ideals that prioritize fair skin and Eurocentric features marginalize individuals of color and perpetuate harmful stereotypes. Similarly, the emphasis on youth and the stigmatization of aging contribute to age discrimination and unrealistic expectations for older adults. These intersecting forms of discrimination highlight the broader societal implications of narrow beauty standards and the need for a more inclusive and diverse representation of beauty.

Addressing the harmful effects of beauty standards requires a multifaceted approach that involves individuals, media, industries, and policymakers. On a personal level, cultivating self-compassion and body positivity can help individuals resist the pressure to conform to unrealistic ideals. This involves recognizing and challenging the internalized messages about beauty and learning to appreciate one's unique appearance and qualities.

Media literacy is crucial in helping individuals critically evaluate the images and messages they encounter. Education programs that teach media literacy skills can empower people to recognize digital manipulation, understand the motives behind advertising, and develop a healthier relationship with media consumption. Encouraging diverse representation in media is also essential. By showcasing a wide range of body types, skin tones, ages, and ethnicities, media can promote a more inclusive and realistic standard of beauty.

The beauty and fashion industries have a significant role to play in challenging harmful beauty standards. Brands and companies can adopt more inclusive marketing strategies that celebrate diversity and authenticity. This includes using models of various sizes, ages, and backgrounds and refraining from excessive digital alteration of images. Some companies have already begun to embrace this approach, but there is still a long way to go in shifting industry norms.

Policymakers can also contribute to addressing the impact of beauty standards by regulating advertising practices and promoting public health campaigns that emphasize the importance of mental and physical well-being over appearance. Policies that address discrimination based on appearance in the workplace and other settings can help reduce the social and economic disparities linked to beauty standards.

Community support and activism are powerful tools for creating change. Grassroots movements that promote body positivity and challenge harmful beauty norms can raise awareness and inspire collective action. Online communities and social media campaigns, such as the body positivity movement, have already made significant strides in shifting public perceptions and encouraging more inclusive standards of beauty.

Educational institutions can play a crucial role in fostering a healthy relationship with body image among young people. Incorporating lessons on self-esteem, body diversity, and media literacy into school curricula can help students develop a more balanced and critical perspective on beauty standards. Providing resources and support for students struggling with body image issues or eating disorders is also essential for promoting mental and physical health.

Ultimately, dismantling harmful beauty standards requires a cultural shift that prioritizes individuality, diversity, and authenticity over conformity to narrow ideals. This involves challenging deeply ingrained societal norms and embracing a more holistic view of beauty that encompasses inner qualities, talents, and the unique characteristics that make each person special. By promoting a culture of acceptance and inclusivity, we can create a society where individuals are valued for who they are rather than how they look, leading to healthier, happier, and more equitable communities.

The journey towards a more inclusive and healthy perception of beauty is ongoing and complex, but it is a necessary endeavor for the well-being of individuals and society as a whole. By addressing the harmful pursuit of perfection and fostering a more inclusive and compassionate understanding of beauty, we can begin to heal the wounds inflicted by rigid beauty standards and move towards a future where everyone is free to be their true selves without fear of judgment or exclusion.

Chapter 12: Privacy Erosion

Privacy erosion is an increasingly pervasive issue in contemporary society, characterized by the gradual and often unnoticed diminishment of individuals' ability to control their personal information and maintain a private sphere. The consequences of living publicly, where personal data is constantly collected, shared, and analyzed, are far-reaching and multifaceted. This phenomenon has been accelerated by the advent of digital technology, social media, and pervasive surveillance practices, leading to significant implications for individual autonomy, security, social relations, and democracy. To understand the depth and breadth of privacy erosion, it is essential to explore its causes, manifestations, and effects in detail.

The roots of privacy erosion can be traced to the rapid advancement and widespread adoption of digital technologies. The internet and mobile devices have revolutionized communication, commerce, and social interaction, creating an environment where vast amounts of personal data are generated and shared daily. Every online activity, from social media posts and search queries to online purchases and location data, contributes to a detailed digital footprint. This data is often collected by tech companies, advertisers, and other third parties who use it for various purposes, including targeted advertising, user profiling, and behavior prediction.

Social media platforms are among the primary contributors to privacy erosion. Platforms like Facebook, Instagram, and Twitter encourage users to share personal information, photos, and opinions publicly, often without fully understanding the implications. The design of these platforms, which rewards engagement through likes, shares, and comments, creates an incentive for users to disclose more about themselves. This culture of sharing blurs the line between public and private life, making it difficult to maintain a clear boundary.

The collection and analysis of personal data by tech companies are facilitated by sophisticated algorithms and artificial intelligence. These technologies can process vast amounts of data to create detailed profiles of individuals, predicting their preferences, behaviors, and even emotions. While this can lead to more personalized services and conveniences, it also raises significant privacy concerns. The extent to which personal data is collected, stored, and potentially misused is often not transparent to users, leading to a loss of control over one's personal information.

Government surveillance is another critical factor in privacy erosion. In many countries, government agencies engage in extensive surveillance practices under the guise of national security, crime prevention, and public safety. The proliferation of surveillance technologies, such as CCTV cameras, facial recognition systems, and data mining software, enables governments to monitor citizens' activities more comprehensively than ever before. While surveillance can enhance security, it also poses risks to civil liberties and individual privacy, creating a climate of constant monitoring and scrutiny.

The consequences of living publicly extend beyond the individual to impact societal structures and democratic processes. One significant effect is the erosion of individual autonomy. When personal data is constantly collected and analyzed, individuals may feel pressured to conform to certain norms and behaviors, knowing that their actions are being monitored. This can lead to self-censorship and a reduction in the freedom to express oneself authentically. The knowledge that one's private life is accessible to others can also create anxiety and stress, undermining mental well-being.

Privacy erosion also has profound implications for security. The more personal information is available online, the greater the risk of data breaches and identity theft. Cybercriminals can exploit personal data to commit fraud, steal identities, and carry out other malicious activities. Even seemingly innocuous information, such as social media posts or location data, can be used to build profiles for phishing attacks or to track individuals. The increasing frequency and sophistication of cyberattacks highlight the vulnerabilities associated with living publicly.

Social relations are also affected by privacy erosion. The omnipresence of social media and digital communication can alter how individuals interact and perceive one another. The pressure to maintain a curated online presence can lead to superficial connections and a focus on appearance rather than genuine relationships. Additionally, the public nature of social media can lead to conflicts and misunderstandings, as private matters become subject to public scrutiny and judgment. The erosion of privacy can strain personal relationships and diminish the quality of social interactions.

The impact on democracy is perhaps one of the most concerning aspects of privacy erosion. In a democratic society, the ability to communicate and associate privately is fundamental to free expression and political participation. When privacy is compromised, it can deter individuals from engaging in political activities or expressing dissenting opinions. Surveillance and data collection practices can be used to target and intimidate activists, journalists, and opposition groups, undermining democratic processes and stifling political discourse.

Moreover, the use of personal data for political purposes, such as targeted advertising and voter profiling, raises ethical and legal concerns. The Cambridge Analytica scandal, where personal data from millions of Facebook users was harvested without consent and used for political campaigns, is a notable example of how data misuse can influence electoral outcomes and public opinion. Such practices can distort democratic processes by manipulating information and exploiting individuals' psychological vulnerabilities.

Addressing the consequences of privacy erosion requires a multifaceted approach that involves individuals, policymakers, and technology companies. On an individual level, people can take steps to protect their privacy by being mindful of the information they share online and using privacy-enhancing tools such as encryption, VPNs, and privacy settings on social media platforms. Educating oneself about digital privacy and security practices is crucial in navigating the digital landscape more safely.

Policymakers have a critical role in establishing legal frameworks that protect individual privacy and hold organizations accountable for data misuse. Comprehensive data protection laws, such as the General Data Protection Regulation (GDPR) in the European Union, set important standards for data privacy and give individuals greater control over their personal information. Such regulations should be enforced globally to ensure that individuals' privacy rights are respected irrespective of geographic boundaries.

Technology companies must also take responsibility for protecting users' privacy. This includes implementing robust data security measures, being transparent about data collection practices, and giving users more control over their personal information. Companies should adopt privacy-by-design principles, where privacy and data protection are integrated into the development of technologies and services from the outset. Ethical considerations should guide the use of personal data, prioritizing users' rights and well-being over commercial interests.

Furthermore, fostering a culture of privacy awareness and respect is essential. This involves public education campaigns, corporate responsibility initiatives, and advocacy by civil society organizations. By raising awareness about the importance of privacy and the risks associated with its erosion, society can build a collective commitment to safeguarding personal information.

Chapter 13: Rethinking Success

The concept of success has long been synonymous with the accumulation of wealth, a notion deeply ingrained in the fabric of modern society. This association is perpetuated by cultural narratives, media portrayals, and societal values that equate financial prosperity with personal achievement, happiness, and social status. However, the idolization of wealth as the ultimate measure of success is a fundamentally flawed perspective that warrants critical examination. The pursuit of wealth as a primary goal often leads to detrimental consequences for individuals, communities, and the environment, necessitating a broader and more holistic understanding of what it means to be successful.

The roots of equating success with wealth can be traced back to historical and cultural developments. In many Western societies, the Protestant work ethic, as described by sociologist Max Weber, emphasized hard work, discipline, and frugality as virtues that lead to material success and, by extension, moral virtue. This ethic laid the groundwork for capitalism, where economic success became a visible sign of personal worth and diligence. Over time, this narrative has been reinforced by the rise of consumer culture, where material possessions and financial achievements are celebrated and admired.

Media and popular culture play a significant role in perpetuating the notion that wealth equals success. From movies and television shows that glamorize the lifestyles of the rich and famous to advertisements that portray luxury goods as symbols of achievement, the media bombards individuals with images and messages that equate financial prosperity with happiness and fulfillment. Social media platforms further exacerbate this phenomenon by allowing users to curate and display an idealized version of their lives, often highlighting material possessions and affluent experiences. This creates a feedback loop where the desire for wealth and the appearance of success become central to one's identity and social standing.

The education system and career pathways also contribute to the emphasis on wealth as a measure of success. From a young age, individuals are often encouraged to pursue fields of study and careers that promise high financial returns, sometimes at the expense of their passions and interests. The pressure to secure well-paying jobs and climb the corporate ladder reinforces the idea that economic success is the ultimate goal. This narrow focus on financial achievement can lead to a competitive and stressful environment where personal fulfillment and well-being are secondary considerations.

While the pursuit of wealth can undoubtedly lead to financial security and access to resources, it often comes with significant trade-offs and unintended consequences. One of the most profound impacts is on mental and physical health. The relentless drive for financial success can result in chronic stress, anxiety, and burnout as individuals push themselves to meet societal expectations and achieve economic milestones. The pressure to succeed financially can also lead to a work-life imbalance, where personal relationships, leisure activities, and self-care are neglected in favor of professional advancement.

Moreover, the idolization of wealth fosters a culture of materialism and consumerism, where individuals measure their worth and success by their possessions and outward appearances. This materialistic mindset can lead to a perpetual cycle of desire and dissatisfaction, as individuals constantly seek more and better material goods to maintain their status and self-esteem. The pursuit of material wealth often fails to provide lasting happiness and fulfillment, as it is based on external validation rather than intrinsic values and personal growth.

The environmental impact of a culture driven by the pursuit of wealth and materialism is also significant. The demand for constant consumption and the production of goods to satisfy this demand contribute to environmental degradation, resource depletion, and pollution. The emphasis on economic growth and consumerism often comes at the expense of sustainable practices and ecological balance, leading to long-term harm to the planet and future generations. The idolization of wealth as success thus perpetuates a system that prioritizes short-term gains over long-term sustainability and well-being.

Socially, the focus on wealth as the primary measure of success exacerbates inequality and undermines social cohesion. In societies where financial prosperity is the ultimate goal, disparities in wealth and income become more pronounced, leading to a widening gap between the rich and the poor. This economic divide can create social tensions, resentment, and a sense of injustice, as those who are unable to achieve financial success feel marginalized and excluded. The concentration of wealth in the hands of a few also undermines democratic principles and the equitable distribution of resources and opportunities.

Rethinking success requires a fundamental shift in values and priorities. It involves recognizing that true success is multifaceted and encompasses various dimensions of life beyond financial wealth. One critical aspect of redefined success is personal fulfillment and well-being. This includes pursuing passions, cultivating meaningful relationships, and finding a sense of purpose and satisfaction in one's endeavors. Personal fulfillment is not necessarily tied to financial prosperity but rather to the alignment of one's actions and values with intrinsic motivations and goals.

Another important dimension is social contribution and impact. Success can be measured by the positive influence and contributions individuals make to their communities and society at large. This includes acts of kindness, volunteering, social activism, and efforts to create positive change and improve the lives of others. A focus on social impact shifts the emphasis from self-centered financial gain to collective well-being and the betterment of society.

Environmental stewardship is also a crucial component of a redefined notion of success. Recognizing the interconnectedness of human well-being and the health of the planet, success can be measured by the extent to which individuals and organizations engage in sustainable practices and contribute to environmental preservation. This involves making conscious choices that reduce ecological footprints, promote conservation, and support the transition to a more sustainable and equitable world.

Spiritual and emotional growth is another vital aspect of true success. This includes the development of inner qualities such as empathy, compassion, resilience, and self-awareness. Emotional intelligence and the ability to navigate life's challenges with grace and integrity are markers of a successful and fulfilling life. Spiritual growth, whether through religious practices, meditation, or personal reflection, can provide a sense of peace, purpose, and connection that transcends material wealth.

To foster a more holistic understanding of success, society must embrace a paradigm shift that values diverse achievements and recognizes the intrinsic worth of individuals beyond their economic status. This involves challenging and changing the cultural narratives and societal structures that prioritize wealth accumulation over other forms of success. Education systems can play a pivotal role by promoting a broader definition of success that includes emotional intelligence, creativity, social responsibility, and environmental awareness.

Media and popular culture also have a responsibility to portray diverse and authentic narratives of success. This includes highlighting stories of individuals who have made significant contributions to their communities, the environment, and personal well-being without necessarily achieving great financial wealth. Celebrating these varied forms of success can inspire others to pursue paths that align with their values and passions rather than societal expectations.

Businesses and organizations can contribute by adopting practices that prioritize employee well-being, social responsibility, and sustainability over short-term profits. Creating work environments that support work-life balance, mental health, and personal development can lead to more fulfilled and productive employees. Corporate social responsibility initiatives and sustainable business practices can demonstrate that success is not solely measured by financial performance but also by positive social and environmental impact.

Policymakers and governments can support this shift by implementing policies that address inequality, promote social welfare, and encourage sustainable development. This includes creating systems that provide equitable access to education, healthcare, and opportunities, as well as incentivizing environmentally sustainable practices and businesses. By fostering an environment where diverse forms of success are recognized and supported, policymakers can help build a more inclusive and resilient society.

Chapter 14: The Charity Paradox

The charity paradox refers to the complex and often unintended consequences that arise when well-meaning efforts to help those in need result in outcomes that are counterproductive or even harmful. This paradox highlights the tension between the intention to do good and the actual impact of charitable actions, revealing the intricate dynamics at play in humanitarian aid, philanthropy, and volunteerism. While charity is driven by the noble desire to alleviate suffering and improve lives, the charity paradox underscores the importance of critically examining and thoughtfully implementing charitable initiatives to ensure they genuinely benefit the intended recipients.

At the heart of the charity paradox is the issue of unintended consequences. These can arise from a variety of factors, including a lack of understanding of local contexts, cultural insensitivity, and the creation of dependency. One common example is the provision of free goods and services, which can undermine local economies. For instance, when foreign aid organizations distribute free food in areas experiencing food insecurity, they can inadvertently disrupt local agricultural markets. Farmers who rely on selling their produce may find it difficult to compete with the influx of free food, leading to decreased incomes and even driving some out of business. This dependency on external aid can stifle local production and self-sufficiency, perpetuating the very problems that the aid was intended to solve.

Moreover, charity can sometimes perpetuate a power imbalance between donors and recipients. This dynamic is often referred to as the "savior complex," where donors, particularly from wealthier countries, view themselves as benevolent rescuers of those in poorer regions. This mindset can foster a paternalistic approach to aid, where the voices and agency of local communities are marginalized. Decisions about what kind of aid is needed and how it should be distributed are often made without meaningful input from those directly affected. This can lead to initiatives that are misaligned with the actual needs and priorities of the communities they aim to help, resulting in wasted resources and missed opportunities for sustainable development.

Cultural insensitivity is another significant factor contributing to the charity paradox. Well-intentioned aid efforts can sometimes clash with local customs, beliefs, and social structures, causing friction and resistance. For example, initiatives aimed at improving health outcomes, such as vaccination campaigns, may encounter skepticism or outright rejection if they are perceived as foreign impositions that do not respect local traditions or practices. Effective charitable work requires a deep understanding of the cultural context and active collaboration with local leaders and community members to ensure that interventions are respectful, acceptable, and sustainable.

The concept of dependency is central to the charity paradox. When aid becomes a long-term fixture rather than a temporary support, it can create a reliance on external assistance that hinders the development of local capacities and solutions. This dependency can erode the resilience and autonomy of communities, making them more vulnerable to future crises. For instance, in regions where international NGOs have been providing basic services for extended periods, local governments and institutions may lack the incentive or capacity to develop their own infrastructure and systems. This perpetuates a cycle of dependency and undermines efforts to build self-reliant and empowered communities.

Additionally, the competitive nature of the charity sector can exacerbate the paradox. Charitable organizations often compete for funding and visibility, leading to a focus on short-term, high-impact projects that generate immediate results and donor satisfaction. This can result in a proliferation of projects that address symptoms rather than root causes, offering temporary relief but failing to bring about lasting change. The emphasis on measurable outcomes and donor-driven agendas can divert attention from more complex and less tangible issues, such as systemic inequalities and long-term development.

The administrative and operational inefficiencies within the charity sector also contribute to the paradox. A significant portion of charitable donations is often consumed by overhead costs, including salaries, marketing, and administrative expenses. This can diminish the amount of aid that actually reaches those in need. Transparency and accountability are critical in addressing these inefficiencies, ensuring that resources are used effectively and that donors have a clear understanding of how their contributions are being utilized.

To navigate the charity paradox and enhance the effectiveness of charitable efforts, several strategies and principles can be adopted. One key approach is the emphasis on community-driven development. This involves actively involving local communities in the planning, implementation, and evaluation of aid projects. By prioritizing the voices and needs of those directly affected, charitable initiatives can be better aligned with local realities and foster a sense of ownership and empowerment. Participatory approaches, such as community consultations and co-design processes, can ensure that interventions are culturally appropriate, relevant, and sustainable.

Capacity building is another critical component of effective charity. Rather than providing temporary relief, aid should focus on strengthening local institutions, systems, and skills to enable communities to address their own challenges in the long run. This might include investing in education, healthcare infrastructure, and economic development initiatives that create sustainable livelihoods. By building local capacity, charity can transition from a model of dependency to one of partnership and empowerment, where communities are equipped to take charge of their own development.

Transparency and accountability are essential for fostering trust and ensuring the effective use of resources. Charitable organizations should commit to clear reporting on how funds are spent, the outcomes achieved, and the challenges encountered. This transparency not only builds donor confidence but also allows for critical reflection and learning. Independent evaluations and audits can provide objective assessments of the impact of charitable initiatives, identifying areas for improvement and ensuring that aid is delivered effectively and ethically.

Collaboration and coordination among charitable organizations can also mitigate the negative effects of competition and fragmentation. By working together and sharing information, organizations can align their efforts, avoid duplication, and address gaps in services. Networks and coalitions can facilitate this cooperation, enabling collective action on complex and systemic issues. Partnerships with local governments, civil society organizations, and the private sector can further enhance the impact and sustainability of charitable efforts.

Ethical considerations should be at the forefront of charitable work. This includes a commitment to respecting the dignity and agency of aid recipients, avoiding harm, and ensuring that interventions do not exacerbate existing inequalities or vulnerabilities. Ethical guidelines and standards, such as those outlined in the Sphere Handbook or the Core Humanitarian Standard, can provide valuable frameworks for guiding the ethical conduct of charitable activities.

Education and awareness-raising among donors and the public can also play a vital role in addressing the charity paradox. By fostering a more nuanced understanding of the complexities of aid and development, donors can make more informed choices about where and how to contribute. This might involve supporting organizations that prioritize long-term development and capacity building, or contributing to pooled funds that allocate resources based on strategic needs and priorities.

Finally, embracing a mindset of humility and continuous learning is crucial for navigating the charity paradox. Charitable organizations must be willing to acknowledge mistakes, learn from failures, and adapt their approaches based on feedback and evidence. This iterative process of reflection and improvement can help ensure that charitable efforts are genuinely effective and responsive to the evolving needs of communities.

Chapter 15: Overmedication

Overmedication is a significant and multifaceted issue that affects millions of individuals worldwide, driven by the powerful influence of the pharmaceutical industry on healthcare practices and policies. This phenomenon is characterized by the excessive and often unnecessary use of medications, which can lead to a range of adverse effects, including drug interactions, side effects, dependency, and diminished quality of life. The pervasive culture of overmedication is fueled by a complex interplay of factors, including aggressive marketing by pharmaceutical companies, the medicalization of everyday life, financial incentives for prescribers, and a healthcare system that prioritizes quick fixes over holistic approaches to health and wellness. To understand the depth and breadth of overmedication, it is essential to explore its causes, manifestations, and consequences in detail.

The pharmaceutical industry plays a central role in shaping the landscape of modern healthcare, exerting considerable influence over both medical professionals and patients. One of the primary mechanisms through which this influence is exerted is through aggressive marketing and advertising campaigns. Pharmaceutical companies spend billions of dollars annually to promote their products, using various strategies to reach both healthcare providers and the public. Direct-to-consumer advertising, which is permitted in only a few countries like the United States and New Zealand, inundates the public with messages that often emphasize the benefits of medications while downplaying potential risks. These advertisements can create a perception that medications are the primary solution for a wide range of health issues, leading to increased demand and expectations for pharmaceutical interventions.

Marketing efforts directed at healthcare professionals are equally pervasive and influential. Pharmaceutical representatives, also known as "drug reps," routinely visit doctors' offices to promote new medications, often providing free samples, sponsored educational events, and other incentives. These interactions can shape prescribing practices, sometimes leading to the preference for newer, more expensive drugs over older, potentially equally effective treatments. Additionally, continuing medical education (CME) programs, which are essential for maintaining medical licensure, are frequently sponsored by pharmaceutical companies. This sponsorship can introduce biases in the information presented to healthcare providers, subtly influencing their clinical decisions.

The medicalization of everyday life is another significant factor contributing to overmedication. Medicalization refers to the process by which non-medical issues are framed and treated as medical problems, often requiring pharmaceutical intervention. This phenomenon is driven by a combination of societal trends, cultural expectations, and the interests of the pharmaceutical industry. Conditions that were once considered part of normal human experience, such as mild anxiety, sadness, or occasional sleeplessness, are increasingly being pathologized and treated with medication. The expansion of diagnostic criteria for various mental health and medical conditions has led to a greater number of individuals being prescribed medications for issues that may not necessarily require pharmaceutical treatment.

Financial incentives within the healthcare system further exacerbate the problem of overmedication. In many healthcare settings, particularly in the United States, the fee-for-service model incentivizes the volume of care provided rather than the quality of outcomes. This model can lead to a higher rate of prescriptions, as doctors are often pressed for time and may find it quicker to prescribe a medication than to engage in lengthy discussions about lifestyle changes, alternative therapies, or non-pharmaceutical interventions. Additionally, some healthcare providers may receive bonuses or other financial incentives tied to prescribing certain medications, further driving the overuse of pharmaceuticals.

The consequences of overmedication are profound and far-reaching. One of the most immediate and visible effects is the increase in adverse drug reactions (ADRs). ADRs can range from mild side effects, such as nausea or dizziness, to severe and life-threatening conditions, such as liver damage, heart attacks, or strokes. The risk of ADRs is particularly high among elderly patients and those with multiple chronic conditions, who may be taking several medications simultaneously, leading to complex drug interactions. Polypharmacy, the use of multiple medications by a single patient, is a common issue in these populations and significantly increases the risk of negative health outcomes.

Dependency and addiction are other serious consequences of overmedication, particularly concerning opioid painkillers, benzodiazepines, and certain stimulant medications. The opioid crisis in the United States is a stark example of how the overprescription of medications can lead to widespread addiction and devastating societal impacts. Initially prescribed for legitimate pain management, opioids have led to millions of individuals developing dependencies, with many subsequently turning to illicit drugs like heroin and fentanyl when prescriptions become unavailable. The resulting public health crisis has led to a surge in overdose deaths, strained healthcare resources, and significant economic costs.

Beyond the immediate health risks, overmedication can also lead to a diminished quality of life for patients. The reliance on medications to manage health issues can overshadow the importance of addressing underlying causes through lifestyle changes, psychological support, and other non-pharmaceutical interventions. Patients may become dependent on medications to manage their symptoms, neglecting other aspects of their health that could provide more sustainable and holistic benefits. Additionally, the financial burden of long-term medication use can be substantial, particularly for individuals without adequate insurance coverage, leading to increased stress and reduced access to other forms of care.

The environmental impact of overmedication is an often-overlooked consequence. The production, disposal, and consumption of pharmaceuticals contribute to environmental pollution, particularly water contamination. Medications that are improperly disposed of, such as being flushed down the toilet, can enter waterways and affect aquatic ecosystems. Additionally, the manufacturing processes for pharmaceuticals can generate chemical waste and emissions, contributing to environmental degradation.

Addressing the issue of overmedication requires a multifaceted and systemic approach. One critical strategy is the promotion of rational prescribing practices among healthcare providers. This involves the use of evidence-based guidelines to ensure that medications are prescribed only when necessary and appropriate. Continuing education for healthcare professionals should emphasize the importance of considering non-pharmaceutical interventions and the potential risks associated with overmedication. Efforts to reduce the influence of pharmaceutical marketing on prescribing practices, such as stricter regulations on drug rep visits and greater transparency in CME funding, can also help mitigate the impact of industry bias.

Empowering patients to take an active role in their healthcare decisions is another essential component of addressing overmedication. Patient education programs can provide individuals with the knowledge and skills needed to make informed choices about their treatment options, including understanding the potential risks and benefits of medications. Encouraging open and honest communication between patients and healthcare providers can help ensure that treatment plans are tailored to individual needs and preferences, rather than being driven by external pressures or assumptions.

Healthcare system reforms are also necessary to address the structural issues that contribute to overmedication. Transitioning from a fee-for-service model to value-based care, which emphasizes patient outcomes and quality of care, can help shift the focus from quantity to quality in medical practice. Policies that support the integration of multidisciplinary care teams, including pharmacists, nutritionists, mental health professionals, and physical therapists, can provide a more holistic approach to patient care and reduce the reliance on medications as the primary treatment modality.

Public health initiatives that address the root causes of health issues can also play a crucial role in reducing overmedication. Efforts to promote healthy lifestyles, such as campaigns to encourage physical activity, balanced diets, and stress management, can help prevent and manage many chronic conditions without the need for medication. Community-based programs that provide support for mental health, substance use disorders, and social determinants of health can also reduce the demand for pharmaceutical interventions by addressing the underlying factors contributing to these issues.

Chapter 16: Social Mobility Myths

Social mobility is often heralded as the bedrock of modern democratic societies, embodying the promise that individuals can rise above their socio-economic origins through hard work and talent. This notion underpins the widely cherished ideals of meritocracy and equal opportunity. However, the reality of social mobility is far more complex and fraught with systemic barriers that perpetuate inequality. The myths surrounding social mobility obscure the true obstacles to achieving genuine equality, necessitating a critical examination of the factors that hinder upward movement in society. This exploration reveals that, despite the rhetoric of equal opportunity, numerous entrenched structural inequalities impede the ability of individuals to improve their socio-economic status.

One of the most pervasive myths about social mobility is the belief in the meritocratic ideal, which posits that individual talent, effort, and determination are sufficient to overcome socio-economic barriers. While meritocracy is an appealing concept, it often ignores the significant advantages and disadvantages conferred by one's background. Socio-economic status at birth profoundly influences access to quality education, healthcare, social networks, and cultural capital, all of which play crucial roles in determining an individual's life trajectory. Children born into affluent families are more likely to attend well-resourced schools, receive better healthcare, and benefit from enriching extracurricular activities and supportive home environments. In contrast, children from low-income families often face overcrowded schools, inadequate healthcare, and limited access to educational and developmental opportunities, creating a disparity that is difficult to bridge through effort alone.

Education is frequently cited as the great equalizer, a pathway through which social mobility can be achieved. However, the reality of educational inequality presents a stark contrast to this ideal. The quality of education available to children is heavily influenced by factors such as geographic location, school funding models, and socio-economic status. In many countries, schools in wealthier areas are better funded and equipped, offering advanced curricula, experienced teachers, and a wide range of extracurricular activities. Conversely, schools in low-income neighborhoods often struggle with insufficient funding, outdated materials, and high teacher turnover. This educational disparity starts early and compounds over time, as students from disadvantaged backgrounds are less likely to have access to advanced coursework, college preparation resources, and guidance counseling. Consequently, these students face significant hurdles in gaining admission to prestigious universities, which are often seen as gateways to high-paying careers and upward social mobility.

Higher education, while a crucial factor in social mobility, also embodies significant barriers that disproportionately affect lower-income students. The rising cost of college tuition, coupled with inadequate financial aid, poses a substantial obstacle for many aspiring students. Even when financial aid is available, it often falls short of covering the full cost of attendance, leaving students to rely on loans that can result in substantial debt. Moreover, the application process itself can be daunting, requiring resources and guidance that are more readily available to students from affluent backgrounds. For those who do manage to attend college, disparities in support services, networking opportunities, and internships further perpetuate inequality. Elite institutions, in particular, tend to offer more extensive career support and alumni networks, which can be crucial in securing desirable jobs post-graduation. Thus, even within the realm of higher education, significant socio-economic barriers persist, undermining the potential for upward mobility.

The labor market presents another formidable barrier to social mobility, characterized by unequal access to job opportunities, wage disparities, and systemic discrimination. Individuals from disadvantaged backgrounds often find themselves in lower-paying, less secure jobs with limited opportunities for advancement. Factors such as educational attainment, social capital, and geographic location play significant roles in determining job prospects. Additionally, implicit biases and discrimination based on race, gender, and socio-economic status further exacerbate these challenges. For instance, studies have shown that resumes with traditionally "white-sounding" names receive more callbacks than those with "ethnic-sounding" names, highlighting the pervasive nature of racial discrimination in hiring practices. Gender disparities also persist, with women and minorities frequently facing pay gaps and limited advancement opportunities compared to their white male counterparts. These labor market dynamics perpetuate existing inequalities, making it difficult for individuals from disadvantaged backgrounds to achieve upward mobility.

Housing and neighborhood segregation are also critical factors that impede social mobility. Residential segregation by socio-economic status and race results in vastly different living conditions and access to resources. Affluent neighborhoods typically offer better schools, safer environments, and more robust social networks, all of which contribute to upward mobility. In contrast, low-income neighborhoods often suffer from high crime rates, inadequate public services, and limited economic opportunities. This geographic inequality reinforces social stratification, as children growing up in disadvantaged neighborhoods face significant obstacles in accessing quality education and employment opportunities. Housing policies and practices, such as redlining and discriminatory lending, have historically contributed to this segregation, creating enduring patterns of inequality that are difficult to dismantle.

Healthcare disparities further exacerbate the challenges to social mobility. Access to quality healthcare is essential for maintaining physical and mental well-being, which in turn influences educational and employment outcomes. However, significant gaps in healthcare access persist, particularly for low-income and minority populations. These disparities result in higher rates of chronic illness, untreated mental health conditions, and lower life expectancy among disadvantaged groups. The high cost of healthcare and insurance, coupled with geographic barriers to accessing medical services, particularly in rural and underserved urban areas, exacerbates these inequalities. Poor health can impede educational attainment and job performance, creating a vicious cycle that hinders upward mobility.

Social capital, or the networks and relationships that individuals can draw upon for support and opportunities, also plays a crucial role in social mobility. Individuals from affluent backgrounds often have access to extensive networks of influential contacts, providing them with information, mentorship, and job opportunities that are not readily available to those from lower socio-economic backgrounds. This disparity in social capital reinforces existing inequalities, as individuals without these networks face greater challenges in navigating educational and career pathways.

Policy and systemic issues also contribute to the persistence of social mobility myths. Welfare policies, tax structures, and labor laws can either mitigate or exacerbate socio-economic disparities. For instance, regressive tax policies that disproportionately benefit the wealthy can widen the income gap, while inadequate social safety nets and support services can leave disadvantaged individuals without the resources needed to improve their socio-economic status. Additionally, labor laws that fail to protect workers' rights and promote fair wages can contribute to the perpetuation of low-wage jobs and economic insecurity.

Addressing the obstacles to true equality and enhancing social mobility requires comprehensive and multifaceted approaches. One critical area of focus is education reform. Ensuring equitable access to quality education from early childhood through higher education is essential. This can involve increased funding for schools in low-income areas, expanding access to early childhood education, and implementing policies that promote diversity and inclusion within educational institutions. Financial support for higher education, such as need-based scholarships and grants, can help alleviate the burden of tuition costs and make college more accessible to students from disadvantaged backgrounds.

Labor market reforms are also crucial in promoting social mobility. Policies that address wage disparities, strengthen workers' rights, and promote equal employment opportunities can help mitigate the structural barriers that hinder upward mobility. This includes enforcing anti-discrimination laws, promoting diversity and inclusion in the workplace, and implementing measures to support job training and career advancement for low-income and minority workers.

Housing and urban development policies must also be addressed to reduce residential segregation and promote equal access to resources. Affordable housing initiatives, anti-discrimination enforcement in housing practices, and investments in underserved neighborhoods can help create more equitable living conditions and opportunities for upward mobility. Additionally, policies that promote mixed-income housing and inclusive zoning can help break down the barriers created by geographic segregation.

Healthcare access and equity are vital components of social mobility. Expanding access to affordable healthcare and addressing the social determinants of health can help ensure that individuals have the physical and mental well-being necessary to pursue educational and career opportunities. This can involve policy measures such as expanding Medicaid, implementing universal healthcare coverage, and addressing healthcare disparities through targeted public health initiatives.

Strengthening social safety nets and support services is also essential in addressing the obstacles to social mobility. This includes measures such as expanding access to childcare, providing income support for low-income families, and implementing job training and placement programs. Policies that promote economic security and stability can help create the conditions necessary for individuals to pursue opportunities for upward mobility.

Finally, fostering social capital and community support networks can help bridge the gap between different socio-economic groups. Mentorship programs, community organizations, and initiatives that promote networking and collaboration can provide individuals with the resources and connections needed to navigate educational and career pathways. Encouraging community engagement and social cohesion can help build a more inclusive society where individuals from all backgrounds have the opportunity to succeed.

Chapter 17: Media Manipulation

Media manipulation is a pervasive and complex issue that has significant implications for public discourse, democracy, and individual understanding of the world. The ability to distinguish fact from fiction in the media is increasingly challenging due to the sophisticated techniques used to influence public perception and behavior. The landscape of media manipulation encompasses a range of strategies, including misinformation, disinformation, propaganda, selective reporting, and the exploitation of cognitive biases. Understanding the mechanisms and effects of media manipulation is crucial for fostering a more informed and critically thinking society.

One of the fundamental elements of media manipulation is misinformation, which refers to the dissemination of false or inaccurate information without malicious intent. Misinformation can arise from errors in reporting, misunderstandings, or the spread of rumors. While not necessarily intended to deceive, misinformation can still have significant consequences, as it contributes to the public's misunderstanding of events or issues. For example, during public health crises, misinformation about treatments or preventive measures can lead to harmful behaviors and increased risks to health.

Disinformation, on the other hand, is the deliberate creation and dissemination of false information with the intent to deceive and mislead. Disinformation campaigns are often orchestrated by individuals, organizations, or governments to achieve specific goals, such as undermining public trust in institutions, swaying public opinion, or disrupting social cohesion. These campaigns can be highly sophisticated, using a mix of traditional media, social media, and other digital platforms to spread false narratives. For instance, during elections, disinformation can be used to influence voter behavior by spreading false claims about candidates or voting procedures.

Propaganda is another critical aspect of media manipulation. It involves the systematic and deliberate promotion of particular ideas, ideologies, or agendas, often by distorting the truth and presenting biased information. Propaganda can be used by governments, political parties, and other entities to shape public opinion and behavior in ways that align with their interests. The techniques of propaganda include the use of emotionally charged language, selective presentation of facts, repetition of key messages, and the creation of an enemy or scapegoat to unite people against a common threat. Historical examples of propaganda include the extensive use of media by totalitarian regimes to control and manipulate the populace, but it is also prevalent in contemporary democratic societies.

Selective reporting and framing are subtle yet powerful tools of media manipulation. Selective reporting involves emphasizing certain aspects of a story while downplaying or ignoring others, thereby shaping the narrative to fit a particular agenda. Framing, meanwhile, refers to the way information is presented and structured, influencing how it is perceived and interpreted by the audience. The framing effect can significantly impact public opinion by highlighting specific angles or perspectives on an issue while obscuring others. For example, news coverage of crime can be framed to emphasize either the severity of the crime problem or the effectiveness of law enforcement, leading to different public perceptions and policy preferences.

The exploitation of cognitive biases is a sophisticated technique used in media manipulation. Cognitive biases are systematic patterns of deviation from rationality in judgment and decision-making. Media manipulators exploit these biases to influence how people perceive and react to information. One common bias is the confirmation bias, where individuals tend to seek out and give more weight to information that confirms their preexisting beliefs while disregarding contradictory evidence. By creating content that aligns with the audience's beliefs, manipulators can reinforce existing attitudes and behaviors. Another example is the availability heuristic, where people judge the likelihood of events based on how easily examples come to mind. Media coverage that repeatedly highlights certain events, such as terrorist attacks or natural disasters, can lead to an exaggerated perception of their frequency and importance.

The digital age has amplified the reach and impact of media manipulation. Social media platforms, search engines, and other digital tools have become central to the dissemination of information. These platforms use algorithms to prioritize content based on user preferences and behaviors, creating echo chambers where individuals are exposed primarily to information that reinforces their views. This phenomenon, known as filter bubbles, can exacerbate polarization and make it more difficult for people to encounter diverse perspectives. Moreover, the anonymity and virality of social media make it easier for disinformation and propaganda to spread rapidly and widely.

Fake news is a term that has gained prominence in recent years, referring to deliberately fabricated stories presented as legitimate news. Fake news can be particularly pernicious because it mimics the format and appearance of genuine news, making it difficult for audiences to distinguish between fact and fiction. The motivations behind fake news can vary, from political objectives and financial gain through clickbait to social engineering and disruption of public trust. The proliferation of fake news has led to widespread misinformation, confusion, and erosion of trust in traditional media sources.

Addressing the challenges of media manipulation requires a multifaceted approach. Media literacy education is a crucial component, equipping individuals with the skills to critically evaluate information and recognize manipulation techniques. Media literacy programs can teach people how to identify credible sources, discern bias, and verify facts. By fostering critical thinking and analytical skills, media literacy can empower individuals to navigate the complex media landscape more effectively.

Regulation and accountability of media platforms are also essential in combating media manipulation. Governments and regulatory bodies can implement measures to hold media companies accountable for the content they distribute. This includes enforcing transparency in advertising, curbing the spread of disinformation, and promoting ethical journalism standards. However, regulation must be balanced with the protection of free speech and the prevention of censorship, ensuring that measures do not infringe on individual rights or stifle legitimate dissent.

Technological solutions, such as fact-checking tools and algorithms designed to detect and flag disinformation, can also play a role in mitigating media manipulation. Fact-checking organizations can collaborate with social media platforms to identify and counter false information, providing users with accurate and verified information. Additionally, advancements in artificial intelligence and machine learning can enhance the ability to detect manipulated content, such as deepfakes and digitally altered images, helping to maintain the integrity of information.

Public awareness and engagement are vital in addressing media manipulation. Encouraging a culture of skepticism and inquiry can help individuals become more discerning consumers of information. Public campaigns that highlight the dangers of disinformation and promote responsible media consumption can contribute to a more informed and vigilant society. Collaborative efforts between civil society organizations, academic institutions, and media outlets can further strengthen the resilience of the public against manipulation.

Chapter 18: Technological Utopianism

Technological utopianism is the belief that advancements in technology will inevitably lead to a perfect society where all of humanity's problems are solved, and everyone can lead a life of abundance and ease. This ideology has been gaining traction as technological innovations accelerate, creating a widespread perception that technological progress is synonymous with social progress. However, this optimistic outlook often overlooks the complexities and potential pitfalls of technological advancement. Misunderstanding the relationship between technology and progress can lead to a range of societal issues, including increased inequality, loss of privacy, ethical dilemmas, and environmental degradation. A critical examination of technological utopianism reveals that while technology can undoubtedly bring significant benefits, it is not a panacea and must be approached with caution and critical thinking.

At its core, technological utopianism is rooted in the Enlightenment ideals of progress and rationality. Proponents of this ideology argue that human ingenuity and scientific advancements can overcome any challenge, leading to continuous improvement in the human condition. This belief has been reinforced by historical successes such as the Industrial Revolution, which brought about significant economic growth and improved living standards for many. In the contemporary era, breakthroughs in fields such as information technology, biotechnology, and artificial intelligence have further fueled the notion that technology is the key to a better future.

One of the most prominent examples of technological utopianism is the vision of the "Singularity," a hypothetical future point when technological growth becomes uncontrollable and irreversible, resulting in unforeseeable changes to human civilization. Advocates of the Singularity, such as inventor and futurist Ray Kurzweil, argue that exponential advancements in artificial intelligence will lead to superintelligent machines that surpass human intelligence, fundamentally transforming society. According to this view, superintelligent AI could solve complex problems like disease, poverty, and environmental degradation, ushering in an era of unprecedented prosperity and well-being.

However, this optimistic perspective often overlooks the potential negative consequences and ethical challenges associated with such technological advancements. For instance, the development of superintelligent AI raises significant concerns about control and alignment. If these machines surpass human intelligence, ensuring that their goals and actions align with human values becomes a critical challenge. There is a risk that superintelligent AI could act in ways that are detrimental to humanity if not properly guided. Additionally, the concentration of power and knowledge in the hands of those who control advanced technologies could exacerbate existing social and economic inequalities.

Another area where technological utopianism may lead to misunderstandings is in the realm of genetic engineering and biotechnology. Advances in CRISPR and other gene-editing technologies have opened up the possibility of curing genetic diseases, extending human lifespan, and enhancing physical and cognitive abilities. While these developments hold immense promise, they also pose significant ethical and societal questions. The prospect of "designer babies," where parents can select desired traits for their children, raises concerns about eugenics and social inequality. There is a risk that such technologies could lead to a new form of genetic classism, where the wealthy can afford enhancements that give them and their offspring significant advantages over others.

Moreover, technological utopianism often fails to account for the environmental impacts of technological progress. The extraction of resources for the production of advanced technologies, such as rare earth metals for electronics, has significant environmental and social consequences. Mining operations can lead to habitat destruction, pollution, and exploitation of labor in developing countries. Additionally, the proliferation of electronic waste poses a growing environmental challenge, as many of these materials are not biodegradable and can release harmful substances into the environment. The energy consumption associated with data centers and blockchain technologies also contributes to the carbon footprint, exacerbating climate change.

The issue of privacy is another critical concern in the context of technological utopianism. The rise of digital technologies and the internet has transformed how we communicate, work, and socialize. However, it has also led to unprecedented levels of data collection and surveillance. Companies and governments can now collect vast amounts of personal information, raising concerns about data privacy and security. The misuse of personal data can lead to identity theft, discrimination, and manipulation. The increasing use of facial recognition technology, for example, has sparked debates about the balance between security and privacy, with concerns about its potential for abuse in authoritarian regimes and its impact on civil liberties.

Technological utopianism also tends to overlook the social and psychological implications of rapid technological change. The pervasive use of smartphones, social media, and other digital technologies has transformed how we interact and communicate, leading to both positive and negative outcomes. On the one hand, these technologies have connected people across the globe, enabling the sharing of information and ideas. On the other hand, they have also been linked to issues such as social isolation, mental health problems, and the spread of misinformation. The pressure to constantly engage with digital platforms can lead to stress and anxiety, particularly among younger generations who have grown up in a hyper-connected world.

In the workplace, technological advancements have led to significant changes in the nature of work and employment.

Automation and artificial intelligence are increasingly capable of performing tasks that were once the domain of humans, leading to concerns about job displacement and economic inequality. While some argue that technology will create new jobs and opportunities, there is also a risk that it will exacerbate existing disparities, as those with the skills to work with new technologies will benefit, while others may be left behind. The gig economy, driven by digital platforms, has also transformed labor markets, raising questions about job security, workers' rights, and the future of employment.

Given these complexities, it is crucial to adopt a more nuanced and critical perspective on technological progress. Rather than viewing technology as an unalloyed good or a guaranteed path to utopia, it is essential to recognize that technological advancements come with both opportunities and risks. To navigate these challenges, a multi-faceted approach is required, one that includes ethical considerations, regulatory frameworks, and public engagement.

One key aspect of this approach is the development of ethical guidelines and principles to govern the use of emerging technologies. Ethical frameworks can help ensure that technological advancements are aligned with human values and priorities, addressing issues such as fairness, accountability, and transparency. For example, principles of ethical AI emphasize the importance of ensuring that AI systems are designed and deployed in ways that are fair, transparent, and accountable, minimizing bias and preventing harm. These ethical considerations should be integrated into the design and development process of new technologies, rather than being an afterthought.

Regulatory frameworks are also essential to address the potential risks and negative consequences of technological advancements. Governments and international organizations have a critical role to play in establishing regulations that protect public interests and ensure that technology is used responsibly. This can include measures to protect data privacy, prevent monopolistic practices, and promote competition. For example, the European Union's General Data Protection Regulation (GDPR) sets out strict rules on data protection and privacy, giving individuals greater control over their personal information. Regulatory frameworks can also address environmental impacts, ensuring that the development and deployment of new technologies are sustainable and minimize harm to the planet.

Public engagement and participation are crucial components of a responsible approach to technological progress. Inclusive dialogue and consultation can help ensure that diverse perspectives are considered in the development and deployment of new technologies. Public engagement can take various forms, including public consultations, citizen assemblies, and participatory technology assessment. By involving a broad range of stakeholders, including marginalized and underrepresented groups, in the decision-making process, it is possible to address concerns and build public trust in new technologies.

Education and awareness-raising are also vital in fostering a more critical and informed public. Media literacy and digital literacy programs can help individuals develop the skills needed to navigate the complexities of the digital age, including the ability to critically evaluate information and recognize manipulation. Education systems should also emphasize the importance of ethical considerations and social responsibility in science, technology, engineering, and mathematics (STEM) education, preparing future generations to address the ethical and societal implications of technological advancements.

Interdisciplinary research and collaboration are essential in understanding the broader impacts of technology and developing holistic solutions. Collaboration between technologists, social scientists, ethicists, policymakers, and other stakeholders can provide a more comprehensive understanding of the potential benefits and risks of new technologies. Interdisciplinary research can also inform the development of policies and practices that promote responsible innovation and address the complex challenges associated with technological progress.

Chapter 19: Overconsumption

Overconsumption refers to the relentless pursuit of more goods and services than are necessary, leading to the depletion of natural resources, environmental degradation, and social inequality. This phenomenon is deeply rooted in modern consumer culture, where economic growth and material wealth are often seen as the primary indicators of success and well-being. However, the unsustainable nature of overconsumption poses significant challenges to the environment, society, and the economy. Understanding the drivers and consequences of overconsumption is crucial for developing sustainable practices and policies that promote a more equitable and resilient future.

The roots of overconsumption can be traced back to the Industrial Revolution, which marked a significant shift in production and consumption patterns. The advent of mass production, technological advancements, and the rise of capitalism transformed economies and societies, leading to unprecedented levels of material wealth and consumer goods. This period also saw the emergence of consumerism, a cultural and economic system that encourages the continuous acquisition of goods and services in ever-increasing amounts. Advertising, marketing, and the mass media played crucial roles in shaping consumer desires and behaviors, creating a culture of consumption where material possessions are equated with success, happiness, and social status.

One of the primary drivers of overconsumption is the desire for social status and identity. In many societies, material possessions are seen as symbols of success, power, and prestige. People often buy goods not just for their practical use but to signal their social status and identity to others. This phenomenon, known as conspicuous consumption, was first described by sociologist Thorstein Veblen in his work "The Theory of the Leisure Class." Veblen argued that individuals engage in conspicuous consumption to display their wealth and social standing, leading to a cycle of constant upgrading and replacement of goods to keep up with societal expectations.

The rise of global capitalism and the expansion of markets have also contributed to overconsumption. Economic systems that prioritize continuous growth and profit maximization encourage increased production and consumption. Corporations invest heavily in marketing and advertising to create demand for their products, often exploiting psychological triggers and social norms to drive consumer behavior. Planned obsolescence, a strategy where products are designed to have a limited lifespan, further fuels overconsumption by encouraging frequent replacement and disposal of goods. This approach ensures a steady stream of sales but also leads to excessive waste and resource depletion.

Technological advancements and the digital age have amplified overconsumption in new ways. The advent of e-commerce, social media, and digital marketing has made it easier than ever for consumers to access and purchase goods. Algorithms and data analytics allow companies to target individuals with personalized advertisements and recommendations, creating a seamless and often irresistible shopping experience. The convenience of online shopping, combined with the constant bombardment of advertisements and social media influencers promoting the latest trends, has led to a culture of instant gratification and impulse buying.

The environmental impact of overconsumption is profound and multifaceted. The extraction, production, and disposal of consumer goods contribute to a range of environmental issues, including resource depletion, pollution, and climate change. The production of goods requires raw materials, such as minerals, metals, and fossil fuels, which are often extracted through environmentally destructive practices like mining and drilling. These activities can lead to habitat destruction, soil erosion, water contamination, and loss of biodiversity.

Manufacturing processes also generate significant amounts of pollution and greenhouse gas emissions. Factories often release pollutants into the air, water, and soil, contributing to environmental degradation and health problems for nearby communities. The transportation of goods, both domestically and globally, relies heavily on fossil fuels, leading to increased carbon emissions and contributing to climate change. The packaging and disposal of consumer goods create additional environmental challenges, as many materials, particularly plastics, are not biodegradable and persist in the environment for centuries.

One of the most visible consequences of overconsumption is the generation of waste. The throwaway culture, characterized by the rapid disposal of goods in favor of newer, more fashionable items, has led to an unprecedented increase in waste production. Landfills are overflowing with discarded electronics, clothing, and other consumer goods, many of which contain hazardous materials that can leach into the environment and pose risks to human health. The proliferation of single-use plastics, in particular, has created a global crisis, with vast amounts of plastic waste polluting oceans, harming marine life, and entering the food chain.

The social and economic implications of overconsumption are equally concerning. The relentless pursuit of material wealth often exacerbates social inequality, as not everyone has equal access to the resources and opportunities required to participate in consumer culture. The pressure to consume can lead to financial stress and debt for individuals and families striving to keep up with societal expectations. In many cases, low-income communities bear the brunt of environmental degradation and pollution resulting from overproduction and waste disposal, perpetuating cycles of poverty and inequality.

Furthermore, overconsumption can erode social cohesion and well-being. The emphasis on material possessions and individualism can lead to a decline in community values and relationships. People may prioritize personal gain and consumption over collective well-being, leading to a sense of disconnection and alienation. The constant pursuit of more can also contribute to mental health issues, such as anxiety, depression, and low self-esteem, as individuals struggle to meet societal standards of success and happiness.

Addressing the challenges of overconsumption requires a multi-faceted approach that involves changes at both individual and systemic levels. One key strategy is to promote sustainable consumption practices that prioritize quality over quantity, durability over disposability, and needs over wants. Consumers can make more conscious choices by supporting businesses that prioritize ethical and sustainable practices, reducing waste through recycling and reusing, and embracing minimalist lifestyles that focus on experiences and relationships rather than material possessions.

Education and awareness-raising are critical in shifting cultural norms and values around consumption. Schools, communities, and media can play vital roles in promoting sustainability and encouraging critical thinking about the impact of consumption on the environment and society. By fostering a culture of mindfulness and responsibility, individuals can become more aware of the consequences of their consumption habits and make choices that align with their values and the well-being of the planet.

Policy interventions are also essential in addressing the systemic drivers of overconsumption. Governments can implement regulations and incentives to promote sustainable production and consumption, such as imposing taxes on environmentally harmful products, providing subsidies for green technologies, and setting standards for product durability and recyclability. Policies that promote circular economy practices, where products are designed to be reused, repaired, and recycled, can help reduce waste and resource depletion.

Corporate responsibility is another crucial component of addressing overconsumption. Businesses have a significant role to play in promoting sustainable consumption by adopting practices that reduce their environmental footprint and prioritize social responsibility. This can include implementing sustainable sourcing and production methods, reducing waste and emissions, and promoting transparency and accountability in their operations. Companies can also shift their focus from selling products to providing services, such as leasing or sharing models, that reduce the need for constant consumption.

Technological innovation can also contribute to more sustainable consumption patterns. Advances in green technologies, such as renewable energy, energy-efficient appliances, and sustainable materials, can reduce the environmental impact of production and consumption. Digital technologies can also facilitate the sharing economy, enabling people to share resources and access goods and services without the need for ownership. For example, platforms for car-sharing, tool rental, and second-hand markets can help reduce the demand for new products and promote more efficient use of resources.

International cooperation and collaboration are essential in addressing the global nature of overconsumption. Many of the environmental and social challenges associated with overconsumption are transboundary issues that require coordinated efforts and shared solutions. International agreements and frameworks, such as the Paris Agreement on climate change and the Sustainable Development Goals, provide a basis for collective action and commitment to sustainable development. By working together, countries can share knowledge, resources, and best practices to address the root causes of overconsumption and promote a more sustainable and equitable future.

Chapter 20: The Overprotective Parent

The phenomenon of overprotective parenting, often referred to as "helicopter parenting," is characterized by parents who are excessively involved in their children's lives, often to the point of micromanaging their activities and shielding them from any potential harm or failure. While these parents typically have good intentions and want the best for their children, their overprotectiveness can inadvertently hinder child development in several critical areas, including emotional resilience, social skills, and independence. Understanding the motivations behind overprotective parenting, its impact on child development, and strategies for fostering healthier parenting practices is crucial for promoting well-rounded and self-reliant individuals.

Overprotective parenting often stems from a combination of societal, psychological, and cultural factors. In contemporary society, there is a heightened awareness of potential dangers, from physical harm to emotional distress, leading parents to adopt a more protective stance. Media coverage of rare but high-profile incidents, such as child abductions or school shootings, can amplify parental fears, making the world seem more dangerous than it statistically is. Additionally, the competitive nature of modern education and job markets can drive parents to become more involved in their children's lives to ensure their success, often at the expense of allowing them to experience failure and learn from it.

Psychologically, overprotective parents may struggle with anxiety or control issues, leading them to overcompensate by closely monitoring and managing their children's activities. These parents might have experienced significant stress or trauma in their own lives, making them more sensitive to potential threats. Culturally, some societies place a strong emphasis on academic achievement and social status, encouraging parents to take a hands-on approach to ensure their children excel in these areas.

While the intention behind overprotective parenting is often to provide a safe and nurturing environment, the consequences can be detrimental to a child's overall development. One of the primary areas affected is emotional resilience. Children learn to cope with stress and adversity through experience. When parents shield their children from challenges and failures, they deprive them of opportunities to develop coping mechanisms and problem-solving skills. As a result, these children may become overly dependent on their parents and struggle to handle stress or setbacks on their own.

A study published in the *Journal of Child and Family Studies* found that children of overprotective parents exhibited higher levels of anxiety and lower levels of self-efficacy compared to their peers. This is because these children often internalize the message that the world is a dangerous place and that they are incapable of navigating it without their parents' intervention. Consequently, they may develop a heightened sense of fear and insecurity, which can persist into adulthood and impact their ability to take risks and pursue their goals.

Social skills and peer relationships are also significantly affected by overprotective parenting. Social interactions and the ability to form and maintain friendships are crucial components of a child's development. Overprotective parents may limit their children's social interactions out of fear that they might get hurt or be exposed to negative influences. This can lead to social isolation and hinder the development of important social skills, such as empathy, communication, and conflict resolution.

Children who are not given the opportunity to navigate social dynamics on their own may struggle to build meaningful relationships and assert their independence. They may also have difficulty understanding social cues and managing interpersonal conflicts, leading to problems in their personal and professional lives. Research published in *Child Development* highlights that children who are given more autonomy and encouraged to engage in social activities tend to have better social skills and higher levels of emotional intelligence.

Another critical area impacted by overprotective parenting is independence and self-reliance. Developing a sense of independence is a fundamental part of growing up. Children need to learn how to make decisions, solve problems, and take responsibility for their actions. Overprotective parents, however, often make decisions for their children and solve their problems, depriving them of the opportunity to develop these essential life skills.

For example, overprotective parents might intervene in school-related issues, such as completing homework for their children or advocating excessively with teachers to avoid any potential negative outcomes. While this might provide short-term relief and success, it undermines the child's ability to take ownership of their learning and face academic challenges independently. In the long run, these children may struggle with decision-making, time management, and self-discipline, making it difficult for them to succeed in higher education and the workforce.

A longitudinal study published in the *Journal of Youth and Adolescence* found that young adults who experienced overprotective parenting during their childhood had lower levels of self-regulation and executive functioning skills compared to their peers. These individuals often reported feeling less competent and more dependent on others, which negatively impacted their academic and career achievements.

Moreover, overprotective parenting can affect a child's physical health and well-being. Children who are constantly monitored and restricted in their activities may miss out on essential physical exercise and the benefits of outdoor play. Physical activity is crucial for the development of motor skills, physical fitness, and overall health. It also provides opportunities for children to explore their environment, take risks, and build confidence in their physical abilities.

The lack of physical activity can lead to a sedentary lifestyle, increasing the risk of obesity, cardiovascular diseases, and other health issues. Furthermore, children who are not allowed to take physical risks may develop an exaggerated fear of physical activities and avoid them altogether. This can limit their opportunities for social interactions and participation in sports and other recreational activities, further contributing to social isolation and a lack of self-confidence.

To address the negative impacts of overprotective parenting, it is essential to promote healthier parenting practices that balance protection with the need for autonomy and independence. One effective approach is to adopt authoritative parenting, which combines high levels of warmth and support with appropriate levels of structure and expectations. Authoritative parents set clear boundaries and rules while encouraging their children to explore, take risks, and learn from their experiences.

Encouraging open communication is a key component of authoritative parenting. Parents should foster an environment where children feel comfortable expressing their thoughts, feelings, and concerns. By actively listening to their children and validating their emotions, parents can build trust and provide guidance without being overly controlling. This approach helps children develop emotional resilience and problem-solving skills, as they learn to navigate challenges with the support of their parents rather than relying on them for solutions.

Providing opportunities for gradual independence is another important strategy. Parents can encourage their children to take on age-appropriate responsibilities and make decisions within a safe and supportive framework. For example, younger children can be given tasks such as choosing their clothes or helping with household chores, while older children can be encouraged to manage their schedules, complete homework independently, and engage in extracurricular activities. By gradually increasing the level of responsibility, parents can help their children build confidence and self-reliance.

Exposure to diverse social environments is also crucial for developing social skills and independence. Parents should encourage their children to participate in group activities, such as sports, clubs, and community events, where they can interact with peers and learn to navigate social dynamics. These experiences provide valuable opportunities for children to practice empathy, communication, and conflict resolution in real-life situations. Parents can support their children by discussing their social experiences and providing guidance on how to handle different social scenarios.

Promoting a growth mindset is another effective strategy for countering the negative effects of overprotective parenting. A growth mindset, as described by psychologist Carol Dweck, is the belief that abilities and intelligence can be developed through effort and learning. Parents can foster a growth mindset by praising their children's efforts and perseverance rather than focusing solely on outcomes. This approach encourages children to embrace challenges, learn from mistakes, and view failures as opportunities for growth.

Incorporating mindfulness and stress management techniques can also benefit both parents and children. Mindfulness practices, such as meditation and deep breathing, can help parents manage their anxiety and develop a more balanced approach to parenting. By modeling mindfulness and stress management, parents can teach their children to cope with stress and adversity in healthy ways. This can reduce the likelihood of overprotective behaviors and promote emotional resilience in children.

Educating parents about the long-term effects of overprotective parenting and the importance of fostering independence is essential for promoting healthier parenting practices. Parenting workshops, support groups, and resources provided by schools and community organizations can help parents understand the benefits of balanced parenting and provide practical strategies for implementing it. By creating a supportive network of parents, educators, and mental health professionals, communities can work together to promote positive parenting practices and child development.

Chapter 21: Cultural Appropriation

Cultural appropriation is a complex and controversial issue that involves the adoption or use of elements of one culture by members of another culture, often without permission or understanding. This phenomenon can manifest in various ways, including fashion, music, language, rituals, and symbols. While some view cultural appropriation as a form of cultural exchange or appreciation, others see it as a form of exploitation and disrespect, particularly when power imbalances exist between the cultures involved. The debate over cultural appropriation touches on themes of identity, ownership, and respect, raising important questions about how cultures interact and influence each other in a globalized world.

Cultural appropriation often occurs when members of a dominant culture adopt elements of a marginalized or minority culture. This dynamic is rooted in historical and contemporary power imbalances, where the dominant culture exerts control and influence over the marginalized culture. For example, when elements of a marginalized culture are appropriated by the dominant culture, they are often stripped of their original context and significance. This can lead to a superficial or distorted understanding of the appropriated elements, reducing them to mere commodities or trends.

One of the primary concerns with cultural appropriation is the issue of exploitation. When elements of a marginalized culture are appropriated without permission or compensation, it can be seen as a form of theft. This is particularly problematic when the appropriated elements have significant cultural, spiritual, or historical meaning. For example, the use of Native American headdresses in fashion or music festivals is often criticized as a form of cultural appropriation because these headdresses hold deep spiritual significance and are traditionally worn by respected leaders within Native American communities. When non-Native individuals wear these headdresses as fashion statements, it can be seen as a trivialization and disrespect of their cultural and spiritual importance.

Furthermore, cultural appropriation can contribute to the erasure of marginalized cultures. When elements of a marginalized culture are appropriated and popularized by the dominant culture, the original creators and practitioners may be overlooked or ignored. This can result in the erasure of the cultural contributions and achievements of marginalized communities. For example, the popularity of certain African American hairstyles, such as cornrows or dreadlocks, among non-Black individuals can lead to a situation where the cultural significance and history of these hairstyles are overlooked. In some cases, the original practitioners may even face discrimination or negative consequences for wearing these hairstyles, while non-Black individuals are praised for their "edgy" or "trendy" look.

The issue of power dynamics is central to the debate over cultural appropriation. When members of a dominant culture appropriate elements of a marginalized culture, they often do so from a position of privilege. This means that they may not fully understand or appreciate the significance of the appropriated elements, nor the historical and contemporary struggles faced by the marginalized culture. This lack of understanding can lead to misrepresentations and stereotypes, further perpetuating harmful narratives about the marginalized culture. For example, the portrayal of Asian cultures in Western media often relies on exoticized and stereotypical depictions, such as the "dragon lady" or the "kung fu master." These portrayals can reinforce simplistic and reductive views of Asian cultures, contributing to the marginalization and discrimination of Asian communities.

Cultural appropriation can also have economic implications. When elements of a marginalized culture are appropriated and commodified by the dominant culture, the original creators and communities may not receive any financial benefit. This can be particularly problematic when the appropriated elements are used for profit. For example, fashion designers and brands that incorporate traditional Indigenous designs or patterns into their collections may profit from these elements, while the Indigenous communities that created them may not receive any compensation or recognition. This economic exploitation can perpetuate cycles of poverty and inequality within marginalized communities.

Despite these concerns, some argue that cultural appropriation can also be a form of cultural exchange and appreciation. In a globalized world, cultures are constantly interacting and influencing each other. This cultural exchange can lead to new forms of creativity and innovation, as individuals draw inspiration from diverse cultural traditions. For example, the fusion of different musical styles, such as jazz, hip-hop, and reggae, has led to the creation of new and innovative genres. Similarly, the blending of culinary traditions has given rise to exciting and diverse cuisines. Proponents of cultural exchange argue that sharing and adopting elements from different cultures can promote understanding and appreciation, fostering a more inclusive and interconnected world.

However, the line between cultural appreciation and cultural appropriation can be difficult to discern. One key factor is the issue of consent and collaboration. When elements of a culture are shared with permission and in collaboration with the original creators, it is more likely to be seen as a form of appreciation rather than appropriation. For example, when artists and designers work directly with Indigenous communities to create and promote traditional designs, they can ensure that the cultural significance and context are respected and that the communities receive appropriate recognition and compensation. This collaborative approach can help to promote cultural exchange while also addressing the concerns of exploitation and erasure.

Another important consideration is the context and intent behind the adoption of cultural elements. When elements of a culture are adopted with a genuine desire to learn, understand, and respect the original culture, it is more likely to be seen as a form of appreciation. This requires individuals to educate themselves about the cultural significance and history of the elements they are adopting and to approach them with humility and respect. For example, learning about the cultural and spiritual significance of traditional Indigenous ceremonies before participating in them can help to ensure that these practices are respected and honored.

However, it is also important to recognize that intent alone is not enough to mitigate the potential harms of cultural appropriation. Even well-intentioned acts of appropriation can still have negative consequences for marginalized communities. For example, wearing a bindi as a fashion accessory may be intended as a form of appreciation for Indian culture, but it can still contribute to the commodification and trivialization of a significant cultural and religious symbol. Therefore, it is important to consider both the intent and the impact of cultural appropriation.

Addressing the issue of cultural appropriation requires a nuanced and multifaceted approach. Education and awareness are crucial for promoting understanding and respect for diverse cultures. This includes educating individuals about the history and significance of cultural elements, as well as the power dynamics and inequalities that underpin cultural appropriation. Schools, media, and cultural institutions can play a vital role in promoting cultural literacy and fostering respectful cultural exchange.

Additionally, promoting cultural sensitivity and accountability within industries that are often implicated in cultural appropriation, such as fashion, music, and entertainment, is essential. This can include implementing guidelines and best practices for ethical cultural exchange, such as obtaining permission and collaboration from cultural creators, providing appropriate recognition and compensation, and avoiding stereotypical or reductive representations.

Industry leaders and influencers can also play a role in promoting cultural sensitivity and setting a positive example for others to follow.

Supporting and amplifying the voices of marginalized communities is also crucial for addressing cultural appropriation. This includes providing platforms and opportunities for marginalized creators to share their culture and tell their own stories. By elevating the voices and perspectives of marginalized communities, we can promote a more inclusive and diverse cultural landscape that respects and honors the contributions of all cultures.

Chapter 22: Fitness Obsession

Fitness obsession, often referred to as exercise addiction or compulsive exercise, is a condition where an individual feels compelled to exercise excessively and prioritizes it above all other activities, even when it leads to negative physical, emotional, and social consequences. While regular exercise is widely recognized for its numerous health benefits, including improved cardiovascular health, weight management, and enhanced mental well-being, an obsessive approach to fitness can lead to detrimental outcomes. This phenomenon is increasingly prevalent in a society that places a high value on physical appearance and athletic achievement. Understanding the causes, symptoms, and consequences of fitness obsession, as well as strategies for promoting a balanced approach to exercise, is crucial for addressing this growing issue.

Fitness obsession can be driven by a variety of factors, including societal pressures, psychological issues, and cultural influences. In many cultures, physical appearance is closely tied to self-worth and social status. The media and advertising industries often promote unrealistic and idealized body images, creating a sense of inadequacy and pressure to conform to these standards. Social media platforms, with their constant stream of images and posts about fitness achievements and body transformations, can exacerbate these pressures by fostering a culture of comparison and competition.

Psychological factors also play a significant role in the development of fitness obsession. Individuals with low self-esteem, body dysmorphic disorder, or eating disorders are particularly vulnerable to exercise addiction. For some, compulsive exercise becomes a way to cope with negative emotions, gain a sense of control, or achieve a perceived ideal body image. The temporary release of endorphins and dopamine during exercise can create a cycle of dependence, where the individual feels compelled to exercise more frequently and intensely to maintain these positive feelings.

Cultural influences, such as the glorification of athleticism and the emphasis on physical fitness as a marker of success, also contribute to the rise of fitness obsession. In some communities, there is a strong cultural expectation to engage in rigorous physical activity and maintain a fit appearance. This can lead to social pressures and the normalization of excessive exercise behaviors.

The symptoms of fitness obsession can manifest in various ways, affecting an individual's physical health, mental well-being, and social relationships. Physically, excessive exercise can lead to overuse injuries, such as stress fractures, tendinitis, and muscle strains. These injuries occur when the body is not given adequate time to recover between workouts. Chronic fatigue and weakened immune function are also common among those who over-exercise, as the body's energy reserves are depleted, and its ability to fight off infections is compromised.

Mentally, individuals with fitness obsession often experience anxiety and depression. The constant pressure to meet exercise goals and maintain a certain body image can lead to feelings of inadequacy and low self-esteem. Exercise becomes a source of stress rather than enjoyment, and the individual may feel guilty or anxious if they miss a workout or do not meet their exercise targets. This can create a vicious cycle, where the individual exercises more in an attempt to alleviate these negative feelings, further exacerbating their mental health issues.

Socially, fitness obsession can lead to isolation and strained relationships. Individuals may prioritize exercise over social activities, family commitments, and work responsibilities. This can result in missed opportunities for social interaction and support, leading to feelings of loneliness and alienation. Relationships with friends and family members may become strained if they perceive the individual's exercise habits as excessive or disruptive.

The consequences of fitness obsession can be severe and far-reaching. Physically, the risk of injury and illness increases, potentially leading to long-term health problems. Mentally, the constant stress and anxiety associated with compulsive exercise can contribute to the development or worsening of mental health disorders. Socially, the isolation and strained relationships can lead to a lack of support and increased feelings of loneliness and depression.

Addressing fitness obsession requires a multifaceted approach that includes education, awareness, and support. Education is crucial for promoting a balanced and healthy approach to exercise. Individuals need to understand the importance of moderation and the risks associated with excessive exercise. Health professionals, fitness trainers, and educators can play a vital role in providing accurate information about the benefits and risks of exercise, as well as promoting healthy exercise habits.

Awareness is also important for recognizing the signs of fitness obsession and seeking help when needed. Individuals who are struggling with compulsive exercise behaviors need to be aware of the potential consequences and understand that it is okay to seek help. Friends, family members, and healthcare professionals should be vigilant for signs of fitness obsession and provide support and encouragement to those who may be affected.

Support is essential for individuals dealing with fitness obsession. This can include professional support from healthcare providers, such as therapists and dietitians, as well as social support from friends and family members. Cognitive-behavioral therapy (CBT) is an effective treatment for exercise addiction, helping individuals to identify and change unhealthy thought patterns and behaviors related to exercise. Support groups and peer networks can also provide a sense of community and understanding, helping individuals to feel less isolated and more empowered to make positive changes.

Promoting a balanced approach to exercise involves encouraging individuals to focus on overall well-being rather than solely on physical appearance or performance. This includes recognizing the importance of rest and recovery, as well as engaging in a variety of physical activities that are enjoyable and sustainable. Mindfulness and stress management techniques, such as meditation and yoga, can also help individuals to develop a healthier relationship with exercise and their bodies.

In addition to individual efforts, broader societal and cultural changes are needed to address the root causes of fitness obsession. This includes challenging and changing the unrealistic and harmful body image standards promoted by the media and advertising industries. Media literacy education can help individuals to critically analyze and question the messages they receive about body image and fitness, reducing the impact of these pressures.

Workplaces, schools, and communities can also play a role in promoting a balanced approach to fitness. This can include providing opportunities for physical activity that are inclusive and accessible to all, as well as promoting a culture of health and well-being that values mental and emotional health as much as physical fitness. Policies and programs that support work-life balance and mental health can also help to reduce the pressures that contribute to fitness obsession.

Chapter 23: The Happiness Trap

The pursuit of happiness is a universal endeavor, deeply embedded in the human experience. People seek happiness in various forms, often believing that it can be attained through certain achievements, possessions, or experiences. However, this quest frequently leads individuals into what is known as the "happiness trap," where the methods employed to achieve happiness result in the opposite effect, leading to dissatisfaction, stress, and a perpetual sense of inadequacy. This phenomenon arises from misconceptions about what truly brings happiness and the cultural and societal influences that shape our understanding of joy. To understand the happiness trap fully, it is essential to explore its origins, manifestations, and the ways in which individuals can cultivate genuine, lasting happiness.

The happiness trap is rooted in several misconceptions about happiness, many of which are perpetuated by societal norms, cultural narratives, and commercial interests. One of the most prevalent myths is that happiness is primarily derived from external circumstances, such as wealth, status, or material possessions. This belief is reinforced by a consumer-driven culture that equates happiness with consumption and success with accumulation. Advertisements, media portrayals, and social norms often depict the acquisition of goods and the attainment of a certain lifestyle as the ultimate path to happiness. As a result, individuals may spend considerable time and energy pursuing financial success, luxury items, or status symbols, only to find that these achievements provide fleeting satisfaction rather than enduring joy.

Another significant misconception is the idea that happiness is a constant state that can be achieved and maintained indefinitely. This belief can lead to the relentless pursuit of pleasure and the avoidance of discomfort or negative emotions. However, research in psychology and neuroscience suggests that happiness is a dynamic and fluctuating experience, influenced by a range of factors including genetic predispositions, life circumstances, and individual behaviors. The expectation of constant happiness can create unrealistic standards and a sense of failure when individuals inevitably encounter challenges or periods of sadness.

The happiness trap is also fueled by social comparison, which is exacerbated by the rise of social media. Platforms like Instagram, Facebook, and Twitter create environments where people frequently compare their lives to the curated and often idealized portrayals of others. This can lead to feelings of inadequacy and the false belief that everyone else is happier or more successful. The pressure to present a perfect image online can further contribute to stress and a sense of disconnection from one's true self and genuine emotions.

The pursuit of happiness through external validation and comparison can manifest in various detrimental ways. One common manifestation is the workaholic culture, where individuals equate professional success with personal worth. The desire to climb the career ladder, earn promotions, and gain recognition can lead to long hours, chronic stress, and burnout. While achieving career goals can provide temporary boosts in happiness, the long-term effects of neglecting personal relationships, health, and well-being often outweigh these benefits. Moreover, the constant striving for professional success can create a cycle of perpetual dissatisfaction, where each achievement is followed by the next goal, leaving little room for contentment.

Another manifestation of the happiness trap is the reliance on material possessions for fulfillment. The phenomenon of "retail therapy" – shopping to improve one's mood – exemplifies this tendency. While purchasing new items can provide a short-term sense of pleasure, it rarely leads to lasting happiness. The novelty of new possessions wears off quickly, and individuals may find themselves caught in a cycle of continual consumption, always seeking the next purchase to fill an emotional void. This can lead to financial stress, clutter, and a sense of emptiness that material goods cannot truly alleviate.

In the realm of personal relationships, the happiness trap can lead individuals to seek validation and self-worth through romantic partnerships or social status. The belief that a perfect relationship or a certain social standing will bring lasting happiness can result in unhealthy dynamics and unrealistic expectations. People may stay in unfulfilling relationships, constantly seek new partners, or prioritize social appearances over genuine connections, ultimately leading to feelings of loneliness and discontent.

The consequences of the happiness trap are far-reaching, affecting mental health, physical well-being, and overall quality of life. The constant pursuit of external sources of happiness can lead to chronic stress, anxiety, and depression. The pressure to achieve and maintain certain standards can result in burnout, physical health problems, and a weakened immune system. Additionally, the focus on external validation can erode self-esteem and create a disconnection from one's true values and passions.

To escape the happiness trap and cultivate genuine, lasting happiness, it is essential to shift the focus from external achievements and possessions to internal well-being and meaningful experiences. One of the foundational principles of genuine happiness is the concept of intrinsic motivation, which involves engaging in activities and pursuits that are inherently rewarding and aligned with one's values and passions. Intrinsic motivation contrasts with extrinsic motivation, which is driven by external rewards and validation. Research has shown that individuals who pursue intrinsically motivated goals, such as personal growth, meaningful relationships, and community involvement, tend to experience higher levels of well-being and life satisfaction.

Mindfulness and gratitude practices can also play a crucial role in fostering genuine happiness. Mindfulness involves being present in the moment and cultivating an awareness of one's thoughts, feelings, and surroundings. By practicing mindfulness, individuals can develop a greater appreciation for the present and reduce the tendency to dwell on past regrets or future anxieties. Gratitude practices, such as keeping a gratitude journal or regularly expressing appreciation for the positive aspects of one's life, can shift the focus from what is lacking to what is already present and fulfilling. Research has shown that gratitude can enhance overall well-being, improve relationships, and increase resilience in the face of challenges.

Building and maintaining meaningful relationships is another key component of lasting happiness. Strong social connections and supportive relationships provide emotional support, a sense of belonging, and opportunities for shared experiences. Investing time and energy in nurturing relationships with family, friends, and communities can create a strong foundation for happiness. Acts of kindness, empathy, and compassion not only strengthen relationships but also contribute to a sense of purpose and fulfillment.

Engaging in activities that promote personal growth and self-care is also essential for genuine happiness. This can include pursuing hobbies and interests, engaging in creative endeavors, and taking care of one's physical and mental health. Regular physical activity, a balanced diet, sufficient sleep, and stress management techniques are foundational to overall well-being. Additionally, setting and working towards personal goals, whether they involve learning new skills, achieving fitness milestones, or exploring new interests, can provide a sense of accomplishment and purpose.

It is also important to redefine success and happiness in a way that aligns with one's values and authentic self. This involves questioning societal norms and cultural narratives that equate happiness with material wealth, status, and external achievements. By identifying and prioritizing what truly matters to oneself, individuals can create a more meaningful and fulfilling life. This may involve making intentional choices about how to spend time and resources, setting boundaries to protect one's well-being, and seeking out environments and communities that support one's values and goals.

Therapeutic approaches, such as cognitive-behavioral therapy (CBT) and acceptance and commitment therapy (ACT), can also be valuable in addressing the happiness trap. CBT focuses on identifying and changing negative thought patterns and behaviors that contribute to stress and unhappiness. ACT emphasizes acceptance of negative emotions and experiences, while committing to actions that are aligned with one's values. Both approaches can help individuals develop healthier perspectives on happiness and create more fulfilling lives.

Chapter 24: Careerism

Careerism, the phenomenon where an individual's life revolves primarily around their career, is increasingly prevalent in modern society. This single-track life path, characterized by an unwavering focus on professional success and advancement, can offer numerous rewards, including financial stability, status, and a sense of accomplishment. However, it also comes with significant drawbacks, such as work-life imbalance, stress, and the neglect of personal relationships and well-being. Understanding the dynamics of careerism, its origins, implications, and ways to achieve a more balanced life is essential in a world where career often dictates one's identity and self-worth.

Careerism can be traced back to various societal, cultural, and psychological factors. Societally, the industrial revolution and the subsequent rise of capitalism placed a strong emphasis on work as a measure of an individual's worth. The notion of the "self-made man" emerged, celebrating those who achieved success through hard work and perseverance. This idea has persisted and evolved, with modern society often equating career success with personal success. The media and popular culture perpetuate this by glorifying high-achievers and presenting an image of success that is closely tied to professional accomplishments and material wealth.

Culturally, many societies place a high value on career and professional success. In the United States, for example, the "American Dream" is often interpreted as achieving upward mobility through one's career. In many Asian cultures, academic and professional success is similarly emphasized, with parents and educators encouraging children to excel in school and secure prestigious jobs. This cultural emphasis on career success can lead individuals to prioritize their professional lives over other aspects of life.

Psychologically, careerism can be driven by various motivations, including the desire for achievement, recognition, and financial security. For some individuals, their career becomes a source of identity and self-worth. They derive a significant portion of their self-esteem from their professional accomplishments and the validation they receive from others. The competitive nature of many industries can also contribute to careerism, as individuals strive to outperform their peers and climb the corporate ladder.

The implications of careerism are far-reaching and multifaceted. On one hand, a strong focus on career can lead to significant professional achievements and financial rewards. Individuals who are dedicated to their careers often excel in their fields, gain recognition, and enjoy the material benefits that come with high-paying jobs. Careerism can also provide a sense of purpose and fulfillment, particularly for those who are passionate about their work and find it meaningful.

However, the single-track life path of careerism also comes with substantial drawbacks. One of the most significant issues is work-life imbalance. When individuals prioritize their careers above all else, other aspects of their lives, such as personal relationships, hobbies, and self-care, often suffer. Long work hours, constant availability, and the pressure to perform can lead to chronic stress and burnout. Physical health can also be affected, as individuals may neglect exercise, sleep, and proper nutrition in favor of work.

The impact of careerism on personal relationships can be profound. Friends and family members may feel neglected or secondary to the individual's career ambitions. The lack of quality time spent with loved ones can strain relationships and lead to feelings of isolation and loneliness. For parents who are career-focused, balancing work and family responsibilities can be particularly challenging, and their children may feel the effects of their absence or preoccupation with work.

Mentally, careerism can lead to a range of issues, including anxiety, depression, and a diminished sense of self-worth. The constant pressure to succeed and the fear of failure can create a high-stress environment. When individuals tie their self-esteem to their professional achievements, setbacks at work can have a devastating impact on their mental health. The pursuit of career success can also become all-consuming, leaving little room for self-reflection and personal growth.

Despite these drawbacks, careerism remains a pervasive force in modern society. The competitive job market and the rising cost of living contribute to the pressure to succeed professionally. Additionally, advancements in technology have blurred the lines between work and personal life, making it increasingly difficult to disconnect from work. Remote work and the expectation of constant connectivity mean that work can intrude on personal time, further perpetuating the cycle of careerism.

Addressing the issue of careerism and achieving a more balanced life requires a multifaceted approach. One key aspect is redefining success to include not just professional achievements but also personal fulfillment, relationships, and well-being. Individuals can benefit from setting boundaries between work and personal life, such as designated work hours and unplugging from work-related communication outside of those hours. Time management techniques, such as prioritizing tasks and delegating responsibilities, can also help in maintaining a healthy work-life balance.

Employers play a crucial role in addressing careerism by promoting a culture that values work-life balance and employee well-being. This can include offering flexible work arrangements, such as remote work and flexible hours, as well as providing resources for stress management and mental health support. Encouraging employees to take regular breaks, use their vacation time, and engage in self-care can also contribute to a healthier work environment.

On an individual level, cultivating a sense of identity and self-worth that is not solely tied to one's career is essential. This can involve exploring interests and hobbies outside of work, building strong personal relationships, and investing time in self-care and personal growth. Mindfulness practices, such as meditation and journaling, can help individuals stay grounded and connected to their values and priorities.

Another important aspect is fostering resilience and a growth mindset. Resilience involves the ability to cope with setbacks and challenges in a healthy way, while a growth mindset encourages viewing failures as opportunities for learning and growth. By developing these qualities, individuals can navigate the ups and downs of their careers without compromising their mental health and well-being.

Educational institutions also have a role to play in addressing careerism by preparing students for a balanced and fulfilling life. This can include teaching skills such as time management, stress management, and emotional intelligence, as well as promoting the importance of work-life balance and self-care. Career counseling services can help students explore diverse career paths and set realistic and holistic goals for their future.

Furthermore, challenging societal and cultural norms that equate career success with personal worth is essential. This involves promoting diverse definitions of success that encompass not just professional achievements but also personal fulfillment, relationships, and well-being. Media and popular culture can play a role in this by showcasing diverse narratives and role models who prioritize a balanced and fulfilling life.

Chapter 25: Housing Market Mania

Housing market mania, often referred to as the housing bubble, represents a period of rapid and unsustainable growth in housing prices, driven by a combination of speculative investment, low interest rates, and lax lending standards. This phenomenon has profound implications for individuals, communities, and the broader economy. The bubble is characterized by a surge in housing demand that outstrips supply, leading to inflated home prices that eventually become unsustainable, resulting in a market correction or crash. To fully understand the dynamics of housing market mania, it is essential to explore its causes, consequences, historical examples, and potential solutions to prevent future bubbles.

The origins of housing market mania can be traced to several interrelated factors. One of the primary drivers is speculative investment, where investors purchase properties not for their utility or rental income, but with the expectation that prices will continue to rise, allowing them to sell at a profit. This speculation can create a self-fulfilling prophecy, as rising prices attract more investors, further driving up prices.

Low interest rates are another critical factor in the formation of a housing bubble. When interest rates are low, borrowing costs decrease, making it more affordable for individuals to take out mortgages and buy homes. This increased affordability can lead to a surge in demand for housing. Central banks often lower interest rates to stimulate economic activity, but if rates remain low for an extended period, it can contribute to asset bubbles, including in the housing market.

Lax lending standards also play a significant role in housing market mania. During a bubble, financial institutions may lower their lending standards to attract more borrowers. This can include offering mortgages to individuals with poor credit histories or requiring little to no down payment. The availability of easy credit can lead to a significant increase in home purchases, driving up prices. The subprime mortgage crisis in the United States during the mid-2000s is a prime example of how lax lending standards can contribute to a housing bubble.

Psychological factors, such as herd behavior and over-optimism, also contribute to housing market mania. Herd behavior occurs when individuals follow the actions of others, leading to a collective rush to buy homes. Over-optimism involves the belief that housing prices will continue to rise indefinitely, causing people to make decisions based on unrealistic expectations. These psychological factors can exacerbate the bubble by driving more people to buy homes, further inflating prices.

The consequences of housing market mania can be severe and far-reaching. When a housing bubble bursts, it often leads to a sharp decline in home prices, leaving many homeowners with properties worth less than their mortgage balances, a situation known as negative equity or being "underwater." This can result in a wave of foreclosures as homeowners are unable to make their mortgage payments or sell their homes for enough to cover their loans. Foreclosures not only harm individual homeowners but also have broader economic implications, including destabilizing financial institutions and reducing overall economic activity.

The burst of a housing bubble can also lead to a broader economic recession. The 2007-2008 financial crisis is a stark example of how a housing market collapse can trigger a global economic downturn. The collapse of housing prices in the United States led to massive losses for financial institutions that had invested heavily in mortgage-backed securities, resulting in a credit crunch and a severe recession. The effects were felt worldwide, leading to job losses, reduced consumer spending, and economic contraction in many countries.

Communities and local economies are also affected by housing market mania. Rapidly rising home prices can lead to a lack of affordable housing, pricing out lower-income residents and contributing to homelessness and housing insecurity. Gentrification, where rising property values displace long-term residents, can alter the social fabric of neighborhoods and lead to a loss of cultural and community identity. When the bubble bursts, the resulting foreclosures and abandoned properties can blight neighborhoods, reducing property values and leading to increased crime and social problems.

Historically, there have been several notable examples of housing market mania and subsequent crashes. The aforementioned 2007-2008 financial crisis was preceded by a period of rapid home price appreciation in the United States, driven by speculative investment, low interest rates, and subprime lending. When the bubble burst, it led to the Great Recession, the most severe economic downturn since the Great Depression.

Another example is the Japanese asset price bubble of the 1980s, where a combination of speculative investment, low interest rates, and lax lending standards led to a dramatic rise in property and stock prices. When the bubble burst in the early 1990s, it resulted in a prolonged period of economic stagnation known as the "Lost Decade."

The housing bubble in Ireland in the early 2000s is another case. Rapid economic growth, speculative investment, and easy credit led to a surge in housing prices. When the bubble burst in 2008, it resulted in a severe recession, with significant declines in property values, widespread foreclosures, and banking crises.

Preventing future housing bubbles requires a multifaceted approach that addresses the underlying factors contributing to housing market mania. One key measure is the regulation of lending standards to ensure that financial institutions do not engage in overly risky lending practices. This includes requiring higher down payments, stricter credit checks, and more rigorous income verification for mortgage applicants. Regulatory agencies can also monitor and limit the issuance of subprime and adjustable-rate mortgages that may pose higher risks to borrowers and the financial system.

Monetary policy plays a crucial role in preventing housing bubbles. Central banks need to carefully manage interest rates to balance the goals of stimulating economic activity and preventing asset bubbles. While low interest rates can boost economic growth, they can also lead to excessive borrowing and speculative investment. Central banks can use macroprudential measures, such as countercyclical capital buffers and loan-to-value (LTV) ratio limits, to mitigate the risk of housing bubbles.

Addressing the supply side of the housing market is also essential. In many cases, housing bubbles are exacerbated by a limited supply of housing relative to demand. Governments can implement policies to increase the supply of affordable housing, such as easing zoning regulations, providing incentives for the construction of new housing, and investing in infrastructure to support residential development. Increasing the supply of housing can help to stabilize prices and reduce the risk of speculative bubbles.

Public education and awareness are crucial in preventing housing bubbles. Educating consumers about the risks of speculative investment and the importance of responsible borrowing can help to curb excessive demand and prevent irrational exuberance in the housing market. Financial literacy programs can teach individuals how to make informed decisions about home buying, mortgages, and personal finance.

Improving data collection and analysis is another important measure. Accurate and timely data on housing prices, mortgage lending, and other relevant indicators can help policymakers and regulators identify potential bubbles and take proactive measures to address them. Enhanced data analytics can also support the development of early warning systems to detect signs of overheating in the housing market.

International cooperation is necessary to address the global dimensions of housing market mania. Housing bubbles and financial crises can have cross-border effects, as seen in the global impact of the 2007-2008 financial crisis. International organizations, such as the International Monetary Fund (IMF) and the Financial Stability Board (FSB), can facilitate the exchange of information and best practices among countries and promote coordinated efforts to enhance financial stability.

Chapter 26: The Gig Economy

The gig economy, characterized by short-term contracts and freelance work as opposed to permanent jobs, has grown significantly in recent years. Many people are attracted to gig work by the promise of independence and flexibility, but beneath this allure lies a complex and often troubling reality.

At first glance, the gig economy appears to offer unprecedented freedom. Gig workers, such as ride-share drivers, freelance writers, and delivery couriers, can often choose when and where to work, theoretically allowing them to balance personal and professional commitments more easily than traditional employees. This autonomy is a powerful draw, especially for those who have grown weary of the rigid structures of corporate employment.

However, this sense of independence is often an illusion. Gig workers typically operate under conditions that undermine the very freedoms that attracted them to this type of work. One of the most significant issues is financial instability. Unlike salaried employees, gig workers do not have a guaranteed income. Their earnings can fluctuate wildly from week to week, depending on demand for their services, competition from other gig workers, and even changes in algorithms used by gig platforms. This unpredictability makes it difficult for gig workers to budget effectively, leading to stress and insecurity.

Moreover, gig workers usually lack benefits that are standard in traditional employment, such as health insurance, retirement plans, paid leave, and unemployment insurance. This absence of a safety net can have severe consequences. For instance, a gig worker who falls ill or is injured might not only lose their income but also face steep medical bills. Without employer-sponsored health insurance, they must either pay out of pocket for healthcare or go without, risking further health complications. The lack of retirement benefits also means that gig workers must save independently for their future, a challenging task given their often erratic income.

Another critical issue is the power imbalance between gig workers and the platforms they rely on. Companies like Uber, Lyft, and DoorDash control key aspects of the working conditions, including pay rates and work availability. They often present themselves as neutral intermediaries connecting independent workers with customers, but in reality, they exert significant control over how work is performed. Algorithms dictate when and where gig workers should be to maximize their earnings, effectively undermining the supposed independence. Furthermore, changes to platform policies or algorithms can happen with little warning, leaving gig workers with no recourse if these changes negatively impact their income or working conditions.

The classification of gig workers as independent contractors rather than employees is another contentious issue. This designation is crucial because it allows companies to evade many legal responsibilities they would otherwise have toward their workers. As independent contractors, gig workers are responsible for their taxes, do not receive overtime pay, and are not protected by minimum wage laws in the same way employees are. This classification has sparked numerous legal battles, with many arguing that gig workers should be recognized as employees entitled to full labor protections.

Additionally, the gig economy can exacerbate social inequalities. Those who rely on gig work often do so because they lack better employment opportunities, which can be particularly true for marginalized groups, including immigrants, people of color, and individuals with lower levels of education. This reliance can trap them in a cycle of precarious employment, with little opportunity for upward mobility. Moreover, the gig economy can erode labor standards across the board, as traditional employers might adopt similar practices to cut costs, further undermining workers' rights and job security.

The gig economy also has broader societal implications. The rise of gig work can lead to a more fragmented labor market, with fewer workers in stable, long-term employment. This fragmentation can weaken labor unions and collective bargaining, reducing workers' ability to advocate for better conditions and pay. Furthermore, the prevalence of gig work can shift social norms and expectations around employment, normalizing the absence of benefits and job security.

Despite these challenges, there are efforts underway to address the downsides of the gig economy. Some jurisdictions have introduced legislation to extend certain protections to gig workers, such as minimum wage laws and access to benefits. For example, California's Assembly Bill 5 (AB5) aimed to reclassify many gig workers as employees, although it has faced significant pushback and legal challenges. There are also movements to create new forms of worker organization tailored to the gig economy, such as worker cooperatives and advocacy groups that seek to provide support and representation for gig workers.

Chapter 27: Financial Literacy

Financial literacy, the ability to understand and effectively use various financial skills, including personal financial management, budgeting, and investing, is a crucial competency that is often overlooked in the traditional education system. Despite its profound impact on individuals' lives, many people grow up without adequate knowledge or skills to navigate the complex financial landscape, leading to a myriad of personal and societal challenges.

From a young age, children are introduced to basic concepts of math and reading, but they seldom receive formal education on financial matters. This gap in education leaves many young adults unprepared to handle real-world financial responsibilities. The consequences of this deficiency are far-reaching, affecting everything from personal well-being to broader economic stability.

One of the most fundamental aspects of financial literacy is budgeting. A budget helps individuals track their income and expenditures, allowing them to manage their money effectively. Without the skills to create and maintain a budget, many people find themselves living paycheck to paycheck, struggling to make ends meet. This situation can lead to unnecessary stress and limit their ability to save for future needs or emergencies. A proper understanding of budgeting can empower individuals to make informed decisions, prioritize their spending, and avoid debt traps.

Speaking of debt, the lack of financial literacy often leads to poor debt management. Many young adults, particularly college students, accumulate significant debt through student loans, credit cards, and other forms of borrowing. Without a clear understanding of interest rates, repayment terms, and the long-term implications of borrowing, they may make decisions that adversely affect their financial health for years to come. High levels of debt can limit career choices, delay major life events like buying a home or starting a family, and contribute to mental health issues.

Investing is another critical area where financial literacy is sorely needed. The stock market, real estate, retirement accounts, and other investment vehicles offer opportunities to grow wealth, but they also come with risks. Many people shy away from investing due to a lack of understanding, missing out on potential gains that could significantly improve their financial security. Conversely, those who attempt to invest without sufficient knowledge may fall prey to scams, make poor investment choices, or fail to diversify their portfolios adequately, leading to substantial financial losses.

Saving for retirement is a specific aspect of investing that deserves special attention. With the decline of traditional pension plans and the uncertain future of social security in many countries, individuals are increasingly responsible for their own retirement savings. Without financial literacy, many people do not start saving early enough, do not save enough, or do not invest their retirement savings wisely. This lack of preparation can lead to financial insecurity in old age, forcing individuals to work longer than they planned or to rely on family and social services.

Financial literacy also plays a vital role in understanding and utilizing financial products and services. From choosing the right bank account to understanding mortgage options and insurance policies, having the knowledge to evaluate these products critically can save individuals money and protect them from predatory practices. Financial institutions often offer complex products with terms and conditions that are difficult to understand without a solid foundation in financial literacy. Misunderstanding these products can lead to unfavorable terms and financial hardship.

Moreover, financial literacy is crucial in the digital age. The rise of online banking, digital payment systems, and cryptocurrencies presents new opportunities and challenges. While these technologies offer convenience and new ways to manage money, they also come with risks such as cyber fraud and market volatility. Being financially literate means not only understanding traditional financial concepts but also being able to navigate the evolving digital financial landscape safely and effectively.

The lack of financial literacy has broader implications beyond individual finances. At the societal level, widespread financial illiteracy can contribute to economic instability. For example, the 2008 financial crisis highlighted how a lack of understanding of mortgage products and the broader financial system contributed to risky borrowing and lending practices. Educating the public on financial matters can help build a more resilient economy, as informed consumers are less likely to engage in behaviors that contribute to economic bubbles and crashes.

Recognizing the importance of financial literacy, various organizations and governments have started to promote financial education. Schools are beginning to integrate financial literacy into their curriculums, and numerous non-profits offer resources and training to help individuals improve their financial skills. Employers are also recognizing the benefits of financially literate employees, offering financial wellness programs as part of their benefits packages.

Despite these efforts, much work remains to be done. Financial education needs to be more widespread and comprehensive, starting from an early age and continuing throughout life. It's not enough to have a one-time course in high school; financial literacy should be a lifelong learning process, adapting to changes in the financial landscape and individuals' evolving financial needs.

Chapter 28: Elder Neglect

Elder neglect is a pervasive and often overlooked issue that affects millions of older adults worldwide. As societies continue to age, with increasing numbers of people living longer lives, the issue of elder neglect becomes even more pressing. This phenomenon, which encompasses a range of behaviors and omissions that result in harm or distress to older adults, is rooted in various social, economic, and cultural factors. Understanding the depth and breadth of elder neglect is crucial for addressing it effectively and ensuring that older adults receive the care and respect they deserve.

Elder neglect can be broadly defined as the failure to meet an older adult's basic needs, which include, but are not limited to, adequate food, clothing, shelter, medical care, and personal hygiene. It can occur in various settings, including private homes, nursing homes, and assisted living facilities. Unlike more overt forms of elder abuse, such as physical or emotional abuse, neglect often involves passive actions or inactions, making it harder to detect and address.

One of the primary factors contributing to elder neglect is the changing family structure and dynamics. In many cultures, older adults traditionally relied on their children and extended family members for support and care. However, with the rise of nuclear families, urbanization, and increased mobility, many older adults find themselves living alone or far from their relatives. This geographical and emotional distance can lead to situations where older adults do not receive the attention and care they need. In cases where family members do live nearby, they may be overwhelmed by their own responsibilities, such as work, raising children, and managing household chores, leaving little time or energy to care for their elderly relatives adequately.

Economic factors also play a significant role in elder neglect. Caring for an elderly person can be expensive, requiring expenditures on medical care, special diets, mobility aids, and sometimes modifications to the home to accommodate disabilities. In many cases, families may struggle to afford these costs, leading to situations where the elder's needs are not fully met. Additionally, professional caregivers, such as those in nursing homes or home care services, may be underpaid and overworked, contributing to substandard care. Low wages and poor working conditions can lead to high turnover rates and burnout among caregivers, which negatively impacts the quality of care provided to older adults.

Cultural attitudes toward aging and the elderly also contribute to neglect. In societies where youth and productivity are highly valued, older adults may be seen as less important or burdensome. This ageism can manifest in various ways, from social exclusion and isolation to inadequate policy and resource allocation for elder care. When older adults are not valued, their needs are more likely to be overlooked or ignored.

Neglect can take many forms, each with serious implications for the health and well-being of older adults. Physical neglect involves the failure to provide necessary food, shelter, and medical care. This can lead to malnutrition, dehydration, untreated medical conditions, and poor personal hygiene. Emotional neglect, which can be just as damaging, involves ignoring the elder's emotional needs, leading to feelings of loneliness, depression, and anxiety. Financial neglect occurs when the elder's financial resources are mismanaged or misappropriated, leaving them unable to afford necessary care and services.

Medical neglect is a particularly troubling form of elder neglect, as it directly impacts the elder's health and longevity. This can include failing to administer medications as prescribed, not seeking medical attention when needed, or ignoring serious health symptoms. Older adults often have complex health needs that require regular monitoring and treatment. When these needs are not met, their health can deteriorate rapidly, leading to serious complications or even death.

Social isolation is both a cause and consequence of elder neglect. Many older adults who are neglected live in isolation, with limited social interaction and support. This isolation can exacerbate physical and mental health problems, creating a vicious cycle where the elder becomes increasingly dependent and their neglect becomes more severe. Conversely, elders who are neglected may withdraw from social interactions due to feelings of shame, depression, or fear, further isolating themselves and making it harder for others to notice and intervene.

Institutional neglect is another critical aspect of this issue. In nursing homes and other care facilities, systemic problems such as understaffing, inadequate training, and poor management practices can lead to neglect. When caregivers are responsible for too many patients, they may not be able to provide the necessary level of attention and care for each individual. This can result in neglected hygiene, untreated medical conditions, and a general lack of responsiveness to the needs and preferences of residents. Institutional neglect can also be exacerbated by a lack of regulatory oversight and enforcement, allowing substandard care to persist unchecked.

Addressing elder neglect requires a multifaceted approach that includes raising awareness, improving caregiver support, enhancing regulatory frameworks, and promoting cultural change. Public awareness campaigns can help to shine a light on the issue of elder neglect, educating people about its signs, consequences, and ways to prevent it. These campaigns can also work to combat ageism and promote more positive attitudes toward aging and the elderly.

Supporting caregivers is another critical component of addressing elder neglect. This includes providing financial assistance, respite care, training, and emotional support for family caregivers, as well as improving wages, working conditions, and professional development opportunities for paid caregivers. By ensuring that caregivers have the resources and support they need, we can help to reduce burnout and improve the quality of care provided to older adults.

Regulatory frameworks also need to be strengthened to protect older adults from neglect. This includes implementing and enforcing strict standards for care facilities, conducting regular inspections, and providing mechanisms for reporting and addressing neglect. Additionally, policies should be developed to ensure that older adults have access to adequate healthcare, housing, and social services, regardless of their financial situation.

Promoting cultural change is perhaps the most challenging but ultimately most important aspect of addressing elder neglect. This involves shifting societal values to recognize and appreciate the contributions and needs of older adults. It means creating communities that are inclusive and supportive of people of all ages, where older adults can remain engaged and active members of society. This cultural change can be fostered through education, media representation, and intergenerational programs that encourage mutual understanding and respect between young and old.

Chapter 29: The Dangers of Pop Psychology

Pop psychology, often characterized by self-help books, online articles, and media personalities that claim to offer psychological insights and solutions, has become increasingly pervasive in contemporary culture. While some of these resources can provide valuable guidance and support, many others oversimplify complex psychological issues, promote unproven methods, and mislead individuals in ways that can be harmful. The allure of pop psychology lies in its promise of quick fixes and easy-to-understand advice, but this can obscure the nuances and rigor required for genuine psychological understanding and improvement.

One of the primary dangers of pop psychology is the oversimplification of complex psychological phenomena. Human behavior and mental health are influenced by a multitude of factors, including biological, psychological, social, and environmental elements. Pop psychology often reduces these complexities into catchy slogans, simplistic theories, and one-size-fits-all solutions. For example, many self-help books emphasize the power of positive thinking or the law of attraction, suggesting that merely changing one's thoughts can transform one's life. While positive thinking can indeed have beneficial effects, it is not a panacea and can overlook deeper issues such as trauma, mental illness, and socio-economic factors that require more comprehensive approaches.

Moreover, the commercialization of psychological advice can lead to the spread of misinformation. Authors and speakers in the self-help industry often prioritize marketability over scientific accuracy. This results in the promotion of methods and ideas that may lack empirical support or be based on anecdotal evidence at best. For instance, many popular self-help books advocate for techniques such as visualization or affirmations without providing robust evidence of their effectiveness. This can lead individuals to invest time, money, and emotional energy into strategies that ultimately do not work, causing frustration and disillusionment.

The self-help industry also tends to commodify personal growth, promoting a culture of incessant self-improvement. This can foster unrealistic expectations and contribute to feelings of inadequacy and failure. The underlying message is often that individuals are not good enough as they are and must constantly strive to better themselves. This relentless pursuit of self-improvement can be exhausting and counterproductive, leading to burnout and decreased self-esteem. Instead of fostering genuine self-acceptance and well-being, this approach can perpetuate a cycle of perpetual dissatisfaction.

Another significant concern is the potential for pop psychology to delay or discourage individuals from seeking professional help. When people believe that they can solve their psychological issues through self-help books or online advice, they may postpone or avoid consulting mental health professionals. This is particularly problematic for those dealing with serious mental health conditions such as depression, anxiety disorders, or PTSD. These conditions often require evidence-based treatments, such as cognitive-behavioral therapy (CBT) or medication, administered by trained professionals. Relying solely on self-help materials can result in inadequate treatment and worsening symptoms.

Pop psychology also frequently fails to acknowledge the importance of individual differences. Effective psychological interventions are often tailored to the specific needs, circumstances, and characteristics of each person. Generic advice may not only be ineffective but also potentially harmful if it leads individuals to adopt strategies that are unsuitable for their particular situation. For example, assertiveness training might be beneficial for someone who is overly passive, but it could exacerbate problems for someone who is already overly aggressive.

The influence of charismatic but unqualified figures in pop psychology further complicates the landscape. Media personalities and influencers with little or no formal training in psychology often gain large followings and dispense advice that can be misleading or harmful. Their success is often based more on their ability to connect with audiences and market themselves effectively than on the validity of their advice. This can create a scenario where popularity is mistaken for credibility, leading people to follow guidance that is not grounded in scientific research or clinical expertise.

The role of social media in disseminating pop psychology cannot be overstated. Platforms like Instagram, YouTube, and TikTok are rife with content creators who share bite-sized psychological tips and tricks. While some of this content can be helpful and engaging, much of it is oversimplified and lacks context. The format of social media encourages brevity and virality, which can lead to the spread of catchy but shallow advice. This can create misconceptions about mental health and well-being, as complex topics are reduced to simplistic soundbites.

Furthermore, the prevalence of pop psychology contributes to the stigmatization of mental health issues. By promoting the idea that personal problems can be easily fixed with the right mindset or simple techniques, pop psychology can imply that individuals who continue to struggle are at fault for not trying hard enough or following the advice correctly. This can exacerbate feelings of shame and isolation, making it even harder for people to seek the help they need.

In addition to these individual-level concerns, pop psychology can have broader societal implications. The emphasis on individual solutions to psychological problems can detract from the need for systemic changes. Issues such as economic inequality, discrimination, and inadequate access to healthcare and education profoundly impact mental health. By focusing on personal responsibility and self-improvement, pop psychology can obscure these larger structural issues and reduce the pressure on governments and institutions to address them. This can perpetuate a cycle where individuals are blamed for their struggles while the root causes remain unaddressed.

Despite these significant criticisms, it is important to acknowledge that not all self-help resources are harmful. Some are based on sound psychological principles and can provide valuable support and guidance, particularly when they encourage self-reflection, mindfulness, and proactive coping strategies. However, distinguishing between useful and misleading self-help can be challenging for the average consumer. This highlights the need for greater public education about psychological science and the importance of critical thinking when evaluating psychological advice.

Efforts to mitigate the dangers of pop psychology should focus on promoting psychological literacy. This includes educating the public about the complexities of mental health, the limitations of self-help, and the value of professional psychological services. Schools, workplaces, and community organizations can play a role in providing accurate information and resources. Additionally, mental health professionals can engage with the media and online platforms to share evidence-based information and counteract misinformation.

Regulation of the self-help industry could also be beneficial. This might involve setting standards for the publication and marketing of self-help materials to ensure that they are based on credible evidence and presented responsibly. While such regulation would be challenging to implement, given the vast and diffuse nature of the industry, it could help to protect consumers from the most egregious forms of misinformation.

Chapter 30: Overconfidence Bias

Overconfidence bias is a cognitive phenomenon where an individual's subjective confidence in their judgments, abilities, or knowledge is greater than the objective accuracy of those judgments, abilities, or knowledge. This pervasive bias can lead to a range of negative outcomes, from personal errors in judgment to large-scale disasters in various domains, including finance, business, and public policy. Understanding the nuances of overconfidence bias is crucial for mitigating its effects and promoting more accurate decision-making processes.

At its core, overconfidence bias involves three distinct manifestations: overestimation, overplacement, and overprecision. Overestimation refers to an inflated belief in one's own abilities or performance. Overplacement involves an erroneous belief that one is better than others. Overprecision is the excessive certainty that one's knowledge or predictions are accurate. Each of these forms of overconfidence can independently or collectively lead to poor decisions and unintended consequences.

Overconfidence bias often begins with a miscalibration between one's perceived knowledge and actual knowledge. This miscalibration is reinforced by various cognitive and social factors. For instance, the Dunning-Kruger effect is a well-documented phenomenon where individuals with low ability in a particular domain overestimate their competence, while those with high ability tend to underestimate their competence. This paradox arises because those with limited knowledge lack the insight to recognize their own deficiencies, whereas those with extensive knowledge are more aware of the vastness of their field and their limitations within it.

One of the primary cognitive mechanisms driving overconfidence is the availability heuristic, where individuals rely on immediate examples that come to mind when evaluating a specific topic or decision. This can lead to overconfidence because vivid or recent memories are often given undue weight, skewing one's perception of reality. For example, if an investor recently profited from a particular stock, they might overestimate their ability to predict the market, ignoring the role of luck or broader market trends.

Confirmation bias also plays a significant role in perpetuating overconfidence. People tend to seek out and favor information that confirms their preexisting beliefs while disregarding or undervaluing information that contradicts them. This selective exposure to information reinforces one's sense of certainty and competence, even in the face of contradictory evidence. In a workplace setting, for instance, a manager might ignore negative feedback about a favored strategy, leading to overconfident decision-making that could harm the organization.

Social and cultural factors further compound overconfidence bias. Societies that value assertiveness and decisiveness may inadvertently encourage overconfident behavior. Leaders and professionals who exude confidence are often rewarded and seen as more competent, regardless of the accuracy of their decisions. This social reinforcement can perpetuate a cycle where overconfidence is not only tolerated but celebrated, leading to systemic issues in various sectors.

The consequences of overconfidence bias are far-reaching and multifaceted. In the financial domain, overconfidence can lead to excessive risk-taking and speculative behavior. Investors who overestimate their ability to predict market movements may engage in frequent trading, often to their detriment. Studies have shown that overconfident traders tend to trade more frequently and with less diversification, leading to poorer investment outcomes. The 2008 financial crisis is a stark example where overconfidence among financial institutions and regulators contributed to risky lending practices and the subsequent market collapse.

In business, overconfidence can result in flawed strategic decisions and failed ventures. Entrepreneurs often exhibit high levels of overconfidence, which can drive innovation and risk-taking. However, this same overconfidence can lead to the underestimation of competition, overcommitment to failing projects, and inadequate contingency planning. For instance, a CEO might push for an aggressive expansion without thoroughly assessing market conditions, leading to significant financial losses.

In the realm of public policy and governance, overconfidence bias can have grave implications. Policymakers and leaders who overestimate their understanding of complex issues or their ability to predict the outcomes of their decisions may implement policies that have unintended and often adverse consequences. The Vietnam War, for instance, is frequently cited as a case where overconfidence in military and political strategies led to prolonged conflict and substantial loss of life and resources.

Personal relationships are not immune to the effects of overconfidence bias either. Overestimating one's understanding of a partner's feelings or needs can lead to miscommunications and conflicts. Overconfident individuals may also be less likely to seek advice or consider alternative perspectives, potentially exacerbating interpersonal issues.

Mitigating the effects of overconfidence bias requires a multifaceted approach. One effective strategy is to foster a culture of humility and continuous learning. Encouraging individuals to regularly question their assumptions and seek feedback can help counteract the tendency towards overconfidence. In organizational settings, promoting diverse teams and inclusive decision-making processes can ensure a broader range of perspectives are considered, reducing the likelihood of overconfident decisions.

Education and training programs that emphasize critical thinking and the recognition of cognitive biases can also be beneficial. Teaching individuals about the common pitfalls of overconfidence and the importance of evidence-based decision-making can improve judgment and reduce error rates. For example, training programs for investors and financial professionals often include modules on behavioral finance, which address overconfidence and other biases that can affect market behavior.

Implementing structured decision-making processes is another effective tactic. Techniques such as scenario planning, where decision-makers consider multiple potential futures, and pre-mortem analysis, where teams envision potential failures of a proposed plan, can help identify risks and uncertainties that might be overlooked due to overconfidence. These methods encourage a more balanced assessment of one's knowledge and capabilities.

In the context of policy and governance, establishing checks and balances, encouraging transparency, and fostering a culture of accountability are crucial. Policies should be subject to rigorous scrutiny and debate, with input from a wide range of experts and stakeholders. This can help ensure that decisions are based on comprehensive analysis rather than overconfident assertions.

On a personal level, individuals can adopt strategies to mitigate their own overconfidence. Keeping a decision journal, where one records the rationale behind significant decisions and their outcomes, can provide valuable insights into one's decision-making patterns and highlight instances of overconfidence. Regularly reviewing and reflecting on these entries can promote more accurate self-assessment and learning.

Moreover, individuals can benefit from cultivating mindfulness and self-awareness. Mindfulness practices, such as meditation, can help individuals become more attuned to their thought processes and biases, allowing them to recognize and counteract overconfidence as it arises. Self-awareness involves acknowledging one's limitations and being open to feedback and alternative viewpoints, which can lead to more balanced and effective decision-making.

Chapter 31: Public Shaming

Public shaming, particularly in the form of cancel culture, has become a pervasive and contentious phenomenon in contemporary society. Cancel culture involves the collective, public call to ostracize individuals or entities deemed to have committed socially unacceptable actions or espoused offensive views. While proponents argue that it serves as a necessary means of holding people accountable, critics contend that it fosters a toxic environment, undermines due process, and can cause disproportionate harm to its targets. Understanding the complexities and consequences of cancel culture requires a deep dive into its mechanisms, motivations, and impacts on individuals and society at large.

Cancel culture is deeply rooted in the concept of public shaming, a practice that has existed for centuries. Historically, public shaming was used as a form of punishment, where individuals were subjected to humiliation in public spaces for their transgressions. The advent of social media has transformed this ancient practice into a digital phenomenon, enabling shaming to occur on a global scale with unprecedented speed and reach. Social media platforms like Twitter, Facebook, and Instagram have become arenas where accusations, judgments, and condemnations are broadcasted and amplified, often leading to swift and severe consequences for the accused.

One of the primary drivers of cancel culture is the desire for social justice. Many individuals participate in cancel culture with the intention of addressing perceived injustices, holding powerful figures accountable, and giving voice to marginalized communities. This aspect of cancel culture can be seen as an extension of activism, where public pressure is used to demand accountability and change. High-profile cases, such as the #MeToo movement, have highlighted how cancel culture can bring attention to systemic issues and force institutions to take action against wrongdoers who might otherwise evade consequences.

However, the motivations behind cancel culture are not always purely altruistic. Social media dynamics often encourage performative activism, where individuals engage in public shaming to signal their own virtue or align themselves with popular opinions. This can lead to a mob mentality, where the primary goal shifts from seeking justice to seeking validation and approval from one's peers. The anonymity and distance provided by digital platforms can also embolden individuals to participate in shaming without fully considering the ramifications of their actions.

The mechanisms of cancel culture are inherently flawed, as they often bypass principles of fairness and due process. In many cases, individuals are judged and condemned based on incomplete or unverified information. The immediacy of social media allows for snap judgments, where accusations can quickly escalate into widespread condemnation without a thorough examination of the facts. This can result in innocent individuals being unfairly targeted, as well as disproportionate punishment for relatively minor offenses. Unlike the legal system, which operates on the presumption of innocence until proven guilty, cancel culture often operates on the presumption of guilt based on popular opinion.

The consequences of being canceled can be devastating and far-reaching. Targets of cancel culture may face significant personal, professional, and psychological repercussions. Loss of employment, damaged reputations, and social ostracization are common outcomes, which can have long-lasting effects on an individual's life. The psychological toll of public shaming should not be underestimated, as it can lead to severe stress, anxiety, depression, and even suicidal ideation. The intensity and permanence of online shaming can make it difficult for individuals to recover or rebuild their lives, as digital footprints are nearly impossible to erase.

Cancel culture also raises important questions about free speech and the limits of acceptable discourse. While it is essential to challenge harmful or offensive speech, there is a risk that cancel culture can stifle legitimate debate and dissent. Fear of being canceled can create a chilling effect, where individuals are reluctant to express controversial or unpopular opinions. This can lead to self-censorship and a homogenization of public discourse, where only certain viewpoints are considered acceptable. The suppression of diverse perspectives undermines the principles of open dialogue and intellectual freedom, which are crucial for a healthy and dynamic society.

Moreover, cancel culture often fails to allow for growth, learning, and redemption. People are complex and fallible, and everyone makes mistakes. The rigid and unforgiving nature of cancel culture can prevent individuals from taking responsibility for their actions, learning from their errors, and making amends. Instead of fostering a culture of accountability and improvement, it can create an environment of fear and defensiveness. Encouraging dialogue, education, and rehabilitation, rather than outright ostracism, can lead to more constructive and meaningful outcomes.

The impact of cancel culture is not limited to individuals; it also affects organizations and institutions. Companies, universities, and other entities often face immense pressure to act swiftly in response to public outcry, sometimes making hasty decisions to appease the crowd. This can lead to policies that prioritize immediate reputational management over fair and thoughtful resolutions. In some cases, institutions may implement overly strict or punitive measures to avoid backlash, potentially infringing on the rights and freedoms of their members.

Cancel culture also intersects with broader societal issues, such as power dynamics and systemic inequalities. The voices that dominate cancel culture are often those with the most social media influence, which can perpetuate existing power imbalances. Marginalized individuals and communities may find themselves disproportionately targeted or silenced, while those with more social capital can navigate or manipulate the dynamics of cancel culture to their advantage. Additionally, the focus on individual transgressions can divert attention from structural issues and systemic injustices, allowing deeper problems to persist unaddressed.

Despite its many drawbacks, cancel culture has brought attention to important social issues and has played a role in holding individuals and institutions accountable. However, it is essential to recognize and address its limitations and potential harms. Developing more nuanced and balanced approaches to accountability and justice is crucial for mitigating the toxic effects of cancel culture.

One potential approach is to promote restorative justice principles, which emphasize repairing harm, restoring relationships, and fostering understanding. Restorative justice focuses on dialogue and collaboration between the harmed parties and the offenders, seeking to address the root causes of harm and find pathways to healing and reconciliation. This approach can provide a more compassionate and effective way of dealing with transgressions, allowing for accountability and growth without resorting to punitive measures.

Another important strategy is to cultivate digital literacy and critical thinking skills. Educating individuals about the complexities of online behavior, the importance of verifying information, and the impact of their actions can help create a more thoughtful and responsible online community. Encouraging skepticism of sensationalist claims and promoting respectful dialogue can mitigate the impulsive and reactionary nature of cancel culture.

Additionally, social media platforms have a role to play in addressing the toxic aspects of cancel culture. Implementing measures to reduce the spread of misinformation, promoting diverse viewpoints, and providing tools for conflict resolution and constructive dialogue can help create healthier online environments. Platforms can also establish clearer guidelines and mechanisms for addressing harmful behavior without resorting to permanent bans or extreme punitive actions.

143

Chapter 32: Food Deserts

Food deserts, often defined as areas with limited access to affordable and nutritious food, are a critical issue affecting millions of people worldwide, particularly in urban and rural low-income communities. Despite the growing awareness of food deserts, the complexity and nuances of accessibility are frequently misunderstood or oversimplified. Addressing food deserts requires a comprehensive understanding of the various factors contributing to food inaccessibility, including socioeconomic disparities, geographic constraints, public policy, and the broader food system.

Food deserts are not merely areas where grocery stores are absent. The term encompasses a range of factors that collectively impede access to healthy food. These factors include the availability of grocery stores and supermarkets, the quality and variety of food offered, the affordability of nutritious options, and the transportation infrastructure that affects how easily residents can reach food sources. The U.S. Department of Agriculture (USDA) defines food deserts based on measures of both income and distance to the nearest supermarket, typically focusing on low-income census tracts where a significant proportion of the population lives more than one mile from a grocery store in urban areas, or more than ten miles in rural areas.

Socioeconomic disparities are at the heart of the food desert issue. Low-income communities are often disproportionately affected, as they may lack the financial resources to attract and sustain grocery stores and supermarkets. The economic model of food retailing prioritizes profitability, which can lead retailers to avoid opening stores in areas perceived as less lucrative. This creates a vicious cycle where the absence of grocery stores contributes to poor dietary habits and health outcomes, which in turn exacerbate socioeconomic disadvantages. For many low-income families, the cost of transportation to distant stores, combined with the higher prices often found at smaller, local convenience stores, makes accessing healthy food even more challenging.

Geographic constraints play a significant role in the creation and persistence of food deserts. Urban areas can be particularly problematic due to the high cost of real estate and the competition for space, which can deter large grocery chains from establishing stores in underserved neighborhoods. Rural areas face different but equally challenging barriers, such as sparse populations spread over large areas, which can make it economically unviable for grocery stores to operate. Additionally, rural areas often lack the infrastructure necessary for efficient transportation of fresh produce, resulting in limited availability and higher costs for fresh food.

Public policy and zoning regulations can either mitigate or exacerbate the problem of food deserts. Policies that support the development of grocery stores in underserved areas, such as tax incentives or grants, can help attract food retailers to low-income neighborhoods. Conversely, zoning laws that restrict the types of businesses that can operate in certain areas, or that favor the development of fast-food outlets and convenience stores, can contribute to the proliferation of food deserts. Moreover, cuts to social safety nets and food assistance programs can worsen food insecurity, making it harder for low-income families to afford nutritious food.

The broader food system also plays a crucial role in shaping food accessibility. The consolidation of the food retail industry, with a few large corporations dominating the market, can limit competition and reduce the incentive for these companies to serve less profitable areas. The industrial food system's focus on processed and packaged foods, which are cheaper to produce and have longer shelf lives, often results in a scarcity of fresh produce in low-income neighborhoods. Additionally, the global nature of the food supply chain means that local food systems can be undermined, reducing the availability of locally grown, fresh food in many communities.

The health implications of living in a food desert are profound. Residents of food deserts are more likely to suffer from diet-related health issues such as obesity, diabetes, cardiovascular disease, and other chronic conditions. The lack of access to healthy food options can lead to a reliance on processed foods that are high in calories, sugar, and unhealthy fats but low in essential nutrients. This dietary pattern contributes to poor health outcomes and exacerbates existing health disparities between low-income populations and more affluent communities. Furthermore, the stress associated with food insecurity can have adverse effects on mental health, compounding the physical health challenges faced by residents of food deserts.

Addressing food deserts requires multifaceted solutions that go beyond simply increasing the number of grocery stores in underserved areas. One promising approach is the development of urban agriculture and community gardens, which can provide residents with access to fresh, locally grown produce. These initiatives can also foster a sense of community and empowerment, as residents take an active role in growing their own food and improving their local food environment. Programs that support farmers' markets and mobile markets can also enhance food access, particularly in areas where traditional grocery stores are not viable.

Improving transportation infrastructure is another critical component of addressing food deserts. Public transportation systems that connect low-income neighborhoods to grocery stores and supermarkets can reduce the burden of travel and make it easier for residents to access healthy food. In rural areas, innovative solutions such as grocery delivery services or cooperative buying programs can help bridge the gap between residents and food retailers.

Education and awareness are also essential in combating food deserts. Nutrition education programs that teach residents how to make healthy food choices on a limited budget can empower individuals to improve their diets even in the face of limited options.

Schools, community centers, and healthcare providers can all play a role in delivering these educational programs and supporting residents in making healthier choices.

Policy interventions are crucial for creating systemic change. Governments at all levels can implement policies that support the development of grocery stores in underserved areas, provide subsidies or incentives for retailers to offer healthy food options, and strengthen food assistance programs to ensure that low-income families have the resources they need to purchase nutritious food. Additionally, policies that support local food systems, such as subsidies for small farmers or incentives for farm-to-table programs, can increase the availability of fresh produce in food deserts.

Corporate responsibility and private sector engagement are also vital. Food retailers and manufacturers can take proactive steps to address food deserts by investing in underserved communities, offering affordable healthy food options, and supporting local food initiatives. Public-private partnerships can leverage the strengths of both sectors to develop innovative solutions and scale successful models.

Ultimately, addressing food deserts requires a comprehensive and coordinated effort that involves multiple stakeholders, including government agencies, community organizations, businesses, and residents themselves. By understanding the complexity of food accessibility and implementing multifaceted solutions, it is possible to create more equitable food systems and improve the health and well-being of all communities.

Chapter 33: The Overlooked Impact of Fast Fashion

Fast fashion, the rapid production of inexpensive clothing in response to the latest trends, has transformed the global fashion industry and consumer habits. While it offers affordable and trendy clothing to a wide range of consumers, the fast fashion model has significant and often overlooked impacts on the environment, economy, and society. These impacts extend far beyond the obvious issues of overconsumption and waste, encompassing a wide range of concerns from environmental degradation and labor exploitation to cultural homogenization and the undermining of traditional fashion industries. Understanding the full extent of these impacts is crucial for fostering more sustainable and ethical fashion practices.

The environmental consequences of fast fashion are perhaps the most visible and alarming. The fashion industry is one of the largest polluters in the world, with significant contributions to water pollution, greenhouse gas emissions, and waste. Fast fashion exacerbates these issues through its emphasis on rapid production cycles and low-cost materials. The use of synthetic fibers, such as polyester, is particularly problematic. Polyester, derived from petroleum, is not biodegradable and releases microplastics into water bodies during washing, contributing to the growing problem of plastic pollution in oceans and waterways.

Water usage in the fast fashion industry is another major environmental concern. The production of clothing, especially cotton garments, is highly water-intensive. It takes approximately 2,700 liters of water to produce a single cotton t-shirt, equivalent to what one person drinks in two and a half years. This excessive water consumption strains local water resources, particularly in arid regions where water is already scarce. Furthermore, the dyeing and finishing processes of textiles involve the use of toxic chemicals that often end up in rivers and lakes, contaminating drinking water and harming aquatic ecosystems.

Greenhouse gas emissions from the fashion industry contribute significantly to climate change. The production, transportation, and disposal of fast fashion garments involve a high carbon footprint. Factories producing these garments are often powered by fossil fuels, and the global supply chain involves extensive shipping and air transport, both of which generate substantial carbon emissions. The push for ever-faster production cycles means that energy consumption remains high, with little room for implementing more sustainable practices.

In addition to environmental degradation, fast fashion has profound social and economic impacts, particularly on labor conditions and workers' rights. The majority of fast fashion production occurs in developing countries where labor is cheap and regulations may be lax. Workers in these regions often face exploitative conditions, including low wages, long hours, and unsafe working environments. The pressure to produce large quantities of clothing quickly and cheaply exacerbates these conditions, leading to numerous violations of labor rights. Tragic incidents, such as the Rana Plaza factory collapse in Bangladesh in 2013, which killed over 1,100 garment workers, highlight the severe human cost of fast fashion.

The economic model of fast fashion also undermines traditional fashion industries and local artisans. By flooding the market with cheap, mass-produced clothing, fast fashion brands drive down prices and erode the market share of local designers and craftsmen who cannot compete with the low costs and rapid turnover of fast fashion. This not only threatens the livelihoods of these individuals but also leads to the loss of cultural heritage and craftsmanship that have been passed down through generations.

Cultural homogenization is another overlooked impact of fast fashion. The global reach of fast fashion brands means that the same styles and trends are promoted worldwide, leading to a homogenization of fashion and a loss of local diversity. Traditional clothing and regional styles are often overshadowed by the ubiquitous presence of fast fashion, diminishing cultural expression and identity. This cultural erasure is particularly detrimental in regions where traditional garments hold significant historical and social meaning.

Consumer behavior and societal attitudes towards clothing have also been significantly altered by fast fashion. The constant influx of new styles and trends encourages a throwaway culture, where clothing is seen as disposable rather than durable. This shift in mindset contributes to the massive amounts of textile waste generated each year. In the United States alone, an estimated 85% of textile waste ends up in landfills or is incinerated, amounting to millions of tons annually. The short lifecycle of fast fashion garments, often worn just a few times before being discarded, exacerbates this waste problem.

Addressing the impacts of fast fashion requires a multifaceted approach involving consumers, industry players, and policymakers. Consumers play a crucial role in driving demand for more sustainable and ethical fashion. By making informed choices, such as purchasing from sustainable brands, supporting local artisans, and prioritizing quality over quantity, consumers can help shift the market towards more responsible practices. Education and awareness campaigns can empower consumers to understand the true cost of their clothing and make more conscious decisions.

The fashion industry itself must also take significant steps to mitigate the negative impacts of fast fashion. This includes adopting more sustainable production practices, such as using eco-friendly materials, reducing water and energy consumption, and minimizing waste. Brands can invest in technologies that improve the efficiency and sustainability of their supply chains, and they can commit to fair labor practices, ensuring that workers are paid living wages and work in safe conditions. Transparency in the supply chain is critical, allowing consumers to make informed choices and hold companies accountable for their practices.

Policymakers have a vital role to play in regulating the fashion industry and promoting sustainability. This can involve implementing stricter environmental regulations, such as limiting the use of harmful chemicals and enforcing waste management standards. Policies that incentivize sustainable practices, such as tax breaks for eco-friendly businesses or penalties for excessive waste, can encourage the industry to adopt more responsible behaviors. Additionally, supporting initiatives that promote fair trade and protect workers' rights can help improve labor conditions in the fashion industry.

Innovative solutions and alternative business models can also contribute to addressing the challenges of fast fashion. The rise of the circular economy, which emphasizes designing out waste and keeping products in use for as long as possible, offers a promising framework for the fashion industry. Practices such as clothing rental, resale, and recycling can extend the lifecycle of garments and reduce the environmental footprint of fashion. Companies like Patagonia and Eileen Fisher are already pioneering circular economy principles, offering repair services, take-back programs, and secondhand sales to keep their products out of landfills.

Community-driven initiatives and grassroots movements are also essential in creating sustainable change. Local fashion movements that celebrate traditional craftsmanship and promote sustainable practices can counteract the homogenizing influence of fast fashion. Community-supported agriculture (CSA) models, which connect consumers directly with local farmers, can be adapted to the fashion industry, creating direct links between consumers and local textile producers. These initiatives can help preserve cultural heritage, support local economies, and promote sustainability.

Chapter 34: Community Disintegration

Community disintegration, characterized by the weakening or loss of social bonds within a community, is a multifaceted issue with deep and far-reaching consequences. It touches on various aspects of social life, including family dynamics, neighborhood cohesion, economic stability, mental health, and even political engagement. The decline of tight-knit communities is often a gradual process influenced by numerous factors, such as economic shifts, technological advancements, urbanization, changing social norms, and policy decisions. Understanding the intricate causes and impacts of community disintegration is essential for developing strategies to rebuild social bonds and foster resilient, supportive communities.

One of the primary drivers of community disintegration is economic change. The shift from industrial to post-industrial economies, characterized by the rise of service-oriented and technology-driven industries, has significantly altered the social fabric of many communities. In the past, local factories and businesses provided not only employment but also a sense of identity and belonging. They were places where social ties were formed and strengthened. As these industries declined or moved to other regions or countries, communities that relied on them for economic stability and social cohesion faced significant disruption. Unemployment, underemployment, and economic uncertainty became widespread, leading to increased stress and social fragmentation. The loss of stable, well-paying jobs undermined the economic foundation of families and neighborhoods, contributing to a cycle of poverty and social disintegration.

Urbanization and suburban sprawl have also played significant roles in the breakdown of community bonds. The migration of populations from rural areas to cities in search of better economic opportunities has transformed social dynamics. Urban environments, with their high population densities and diverse demographics, can be more challenging for fostering close-knit communities. People often lead busy, transient lives, moving frequently for jobs or better living conditions. This mobility makes it difficult to establish long-term relationships and a strong sense of community. Furthermore, suburban sprawl, characterized by the spread of low-density residential areas, has led to the physical separation of people. Suburban neighborhoods, often designed with an emphasis on privacy and individual space, lack the communal spaces that encourage social interaction, such as parks, plazas, and local shops. The reliance on cars for transportation in these areas further isolates individuals, reducing opportunities for spontaneous social encounters.

Technological advancements, particularly in communication and entertainment, have profoundly impacted social interactions and community cohesion. While technology has made it easier to connect with others globally, it has also contributed to the decline of face-to-face interactions within local communities. Social media platforms and online communication tools, while providing the illusion of connection, often lead to superficial interactions that lack the depth and richness of in-person relationships. The rise of digital entertainment, such as streaming services and video games, has also led to increased time spent in isolation, reducing participation in communal activities and local events. The decline of local media, such as community newspapers, has further eroded the sense of local identity and shared experience, as people increasingly consume national or global news tailored to individual preferences rather than local issues that affect their community.

Changing social norms and family structures have also contributed to community disintegration. The traditional nuclear family model, once the cornerstone of many communities, has evolved significantly. Increasing rates of divorce, single-parent households, and dual-income families have changed the dynamics of family life. While these changes reflect greater social acceptance and the pursuit of individual fulfillment, they have also led to challenges in maintaining strong family bonds and community ties. The time and energy required to balance work and family responsibilities often leave little room for community involvement. Additionally, the increasing emphasis on individualism and personal achievement can sometimes overshadow the value of collective well-being and mutual support.

Public policy and urban planning decisions have also played a crucial role in either fostering or hindering community cohesion. Policies that prioritize economic development and infrastructure over social well-being can inadvertently contribute to community disintegration. For example, the construction of highways and large-scale developments often leads to the displacement of established communities and the disruption of social networks. Gentrification, while revitalizing urban areas, can also result in the displacement of long-term residents, breaking up social bonds and eroding the cultural fabric of neighborhoods. Conversely, policies that invest in affordable housing, public transportation, and community spaces can help strengthen social bonds by providing the physical infrastructure that supports social interaction and inclusion.

The consequences of community disintegration are profound and wide-ranging. One of the most significant impacts is on mental health. Social isolation and the lack of supportive relationships are strongly linked to mental health issues such as depression, anxiety, and substance abuse. The absence of a supportive community can exacerbate feelings of loneliness and helplessness, leading to a decline in overall well-being. Research has shown that individuals with strong social ties are more resilient to stress and have better health outcomes, highlighting the importance of community for mental health.

Community disintegration also affects physical health. Studies have found that social isolation and the lack of community support are associated with higher rates of chronic illnesses, such as cardiovascular disease and diabetes. Communities with weak social bonds often lack the resources and infrastructure to support healthy lifestyles, such as access to recreational facilities, healthy food options, and healthcare services. The absence of social networks can also reduce the effectiveness of public health initiatives, as people are less likely to engage in health-promoting behaviors without the encouragement and support of their community.

Economic stability is another area significantly impacted by community disintegration. Strong communities often have robust local economies, with businesses that provide employment and services to residents. As communities disintegrate, local economies can suffer, leading to a decline in job opportunities and economic resilience. The loss of social capital, the networks of relationships that facilitate cooperation and economic transactions, can hinder economic development and innovation. In contrast, communities with strong social bonds are better equipped to support local businesses, attract investment, and adapt to economic changes.

The decline of community cohesion also has implications for civic engagement and political participation. Communities with strong social bonds tend to have higher levels of civic engagement, as residents feel a sense of responsibility and connection to their community. They are more likely to vote, participate in local governance, and engage in community organizing. In contrast, communities experiencing disintegration often see a decline in civic participation, as individuals become disengaged and disconnected from local issues. This erosion of civic engagement can undermine democratic processes and reduce the effectiveness of local governance.

Addressing community disintegration requires a multifaceted approach that involves individuals, communities, and policymakers. At the individual level, fostering strong social bonds involves making intentional efforts to connect with neighbors, participate in community activities, and support local initiatives. Building relationships and creating a sense of belonging can counteract the isolation and fragmentation that contribute to community disintegration.

Communities themselves can take proactive steps to strengthen social bonds and promote cohesion. This includes creating and maintaining communal spaces, such as parks, community centers, and local markets, where people can gather and interact. Community-led initiatives, such as neighborhood associations, volunteer groups, and cultural events, can provide opportunities for residents to connect and collaborate. Investing in local institutions, such as schools, libraries, and healthcare facilities, can also support community cohesion by providing essential services and fostering a sense of shared responsibility.

Policymakers play a crucial role in creating the conditions that support strong communities. This involves implementing policies that prioritize social well-being, such as affordable housing, public transportation, and access to healthcare and education. Urban planning decisions should consider the social impacts of development, ensuring that infrastructure projects enhance rather than disrupt community cohesion. Policies that support local economies, such as grants for small businesses and initiatives to attract investment to underserved areas, can help strengthen the economic foundation of communities.

Furthermore, addressing the root causes of economic inequality is essential for preventing community disintegration. Policies that promote fair wages, job security, and access to education and training can help create more equitable and resilient communities. Social safety nets, such as unemployment benefits and affordable childcare, can provide the support that families need to participate in community life and maintain strong social bonds.

Chapter 35: Patriarchy and Gender Norms

Patriarchy and gender norms are deeply ingrained in society, subtly shaping behaviors, expectations, and opportunities for individuals based on their gender. This systemic issue, often perpetuated unconsciously, impacts various aspects of life, from family dynamics and education to professional environments and media representation. Understanding the subtleties of this perpetuation is crucial to addressing and ultimately dismantling the structures that uphold gender inequality.

At its core, patriarchy is a social system in which men hold primary power and dominate in roles of political leadership, moral authority, social privilege, and control of property. Historically, this system has been justified through various means, including legal frameworks, cultural norms, and religious teachings. Even as overt patriarchal practices have been challenged and dismantled in many parts of the world, the underlying norms and expectations continue to influence societal behavior in more covert ways.

One of the primary ways patriarchy persists is through the reinforcement of traditional gender roles. From a young age, children are socialized into specific roles based on their gender. Boys are often encouraged to be assertive, competitive, and independent, while girls are steered towards being nurturing, cooperative, and passive. These early influences shape their self-perceptions and aspirations, limiting the potential for both genders to explore interests and careers outside these prescribed norms. This early socialization is evident in how toys, activities, and even colors are marketed and presented to children, with boys typically receiving toys that promote action and problem-solving, while girls receive toys that focus on beauty and caregiving.

In educational settings, gender norms continue to play a significant role. Teachers, often unconsciously, may encourage boys to take on leadership roles in classroom activities while expecting girls to be more passive participants. Studies have shown that teachers may call on boys more frequently in class, give them more attention, and provide more detailed feedback on their work. This differential treatment can affect self-esteem and academic performance, reinforcing the belief that boys are more suited for certain subjects, such as math and science, while girls are better in humanities and arts. Consequently, these gendered perceptions influence the academic and career choices that students make, perpetuating gender imbalances in various professional fields.

In the workplace, patriarchal norms manifest in several ways, including the gender pay gap, glass ceiling, and work-life balance expectations. Women, despite having the same qualifications and experience as their male counterparts, often receive lower salaries and fewer promotions. The glass ceiling effect restricts women's advancement to higher-level positions, often due to biases that perceive men as more capable leaders. Furthermore, societal expectations around family and caregiving disproportionately impact women, who are more likely to take on part-time work or career breaks to manage household responsibilities. These choices, influenced by societal norms, further limit women's professional growth and economic independence.

Media representation plays a critical role in perpetuating gender norms and reinforcing patriarchal values. Television, movies, advertising, and social media often depict women and men in stereotypical roles. Women are frequently portrayed as objects of beauty and desire, while men are shown as strong, dominant, and authoritative. These representations shape public perceptions and reinforce gender stereotypes, making it difficult for individuals to see beyond traditional roles. The lack of diverse and nuanced portrayals of both genders in media further entrenches these norms, limiting society's imagination of what men and women can achieve.

In addition to media, everyday language and communication patterns reflect and reinforce patriarchal norms. Language often prioritizes male experiences and perspectives, with terms like "mankind" or "chairman" being common in everyday speech. The use of gendered language subtly enforces the idea that male is the default or norm, while female is the exception. Moreover, communication styles that are assertive and direct are often valued and associated with masculinity, while those that are collaborative and empathetic are devalued and associated with femininity. This disparity in communication styles can impact how individuals are perceived and respected in professional and social contexts.

Social institutions, including legal and political systems, also play a role in perpetuating patriarchy. Laws and policies historically created by male-dominated governments often reflect and reinforce patriarchal values. Although significant progress has been made in promoting gender equality through legal reforms, gaps and biases still exist. For instance, laws around maternity and paternity leave often reinforce the idea that childcare is primarily the mother's responsibility. Political representation remains skewed, with women being underrepresented in most governmental bodies, limiting the ability to create and enforce policies that address gender inequality effectively.

The subtle perpetuation of patriarchy and gender norms is also evident in personal relationships and family structures. Traditional family models, which place men as breadwinners and women as homemakers, continue to influence how households are organized and responsibilities are divided. Even in dual-income families, women often bear a disproportionate share of domestic chores and child-rearing responsibilities. These expectations not only limit women's professional opportunities but also reinforce the notion that men should be providers and women should be caregivers.

To address the subtle perpetuation of patriarchy and gender norms, it is essential to promote awareness and education. Challenging stereotypes and biases through educational programs, media campaigns, and public discourse can help shift societal perceptions. Encouraging diverse and inclusive representations in media, implementing policies that promote gender equality in the workplace, and fostering environments where both boys and girls can pursue their interests without constraint are crucial steps.

Additionally, advocating for legal reforms that address gender biases, supporting political representation for women, and promoting shared domestic responsibilities can help dismantle patriarchal structures. It is also important to engage men and boys in conversations about gender equality, encouraging them to challenge traditional norms and support a more equitable society.

The subtle perpetuation of patriarchy and gender norms is a complex issue that requires concerted efforts from individuals, communities, and institutions. By recognizing and addressing the ways in which these norms are ingrained in society, it is possible to create a more inclusive and equitable world for all genders.

Chapter 36: Inequities in Justice

Inequities in justice systems across the world represent a profound and persistent issue that undermines the very foundation of societal trust in legal institutions. The ideal of justice is often symbolized by Lady Justice, who is depicted as blindfolded to signify impartiality, with scales to weigh evidence fairly and a sword to enforce the law. However, in practice, justice is far from blind, and inequities pervade every stage of the legal process. These inequities create an illusion of fairness, masking systemic biases that disproportionately affect marginalized communities.

One of the most significant factors contributing to inequities in justice is socio-economic status. Individuals from lower-income backgrounds face numerous disadvantages in the legal system. They are less likely to afford competent legal representation, leading to higher rates of public defenders, who, despite their best efforts, are often overworked and under-resourced. This disparity in representation can result in poorer legal outcomes, including higher rates of conviction and harsher sentences. Wealthier defendants, on the other hand, can afford experienced attorneys who can navigate the complexities of the legal system more effectively, negotiate better plea deals, and mount more robust defenses.

Racial and ethnic biases also play a critical role in perpetuating inequities in justice. Studies have consistently shown that people of color, particularly Black and Latino individuals, are disproportionately targeted by law enforcement. They are more likely to be stopped, searched, arrested, and charged with crimes than their white counterparts. This disparity is often rooted in racial profiling and implicit biases that influence the decisions of police officers. Once in the legal system, racial minorities face higher rates of conviction and longer sentences compared to white individuals for the same offenses.

These disparities are not only a reflection of individual prejudices but also systemic issues that permeate the entire justice system.

The process of jury selection further highlights the illusion of fairness in the justice system. Although the right to a trial by a jury of one's peers is a cornerstone of many legal systems, the composition of juries often lacks diversity. Prosecutors and defense attorneys have the ability to dismiss potential jurors through peremptory challenges, and there is evidence that these challenges are sometimes used to exclude individuals based on race, gender, or socio-economic status. The resulting lack of diversity can influence the jury's perspective and the fairness of the trial, as jurors from different backgrounds may bring unique viewpoints and experiences that can impact deliberations and verdicts.

Disparities in sentencing reveal another layer of inequity. Mandatory minimum sentences, three-strikes laws, and other punitive measures disproportionately impact minority and low-income individuals. These policies often eliminate judicial discretion, leading to excessively harsh penalties for relatively minor offenses. The war on drugs, for example, has led to the mass incarceration of Black and Latino individuals for non-violent drug offenses, despite similar rates of drug use across racial groups. The long-term consequences of these sentences extend beyond the individual, affecting families and communities through lost income, broken family structures, and diminished opportunities for social and economic mobility.

The issue of wrongful convictions further exposes the flaws in the justice system. Many wrongful convictions have been attributed to factors such as mistaken identity, false confessions, prosecutorial misconduct, and inadequate legal representation. Marginalized individuals are particularly vulnerable to these injustices due to systemic biases and lack of resources. Organizations like the Innocence Project have highlighted numerous cases where new evidence, often through DNA testing, has exonerated individuals who spent years, sometimes decades, in prison for crimes they did not commit. These cases underscore the fallibility of the justice system and the severe impact of its failures.

The conditions within prisons and the broader carceral system also reflect deep inequities. Prisons are disproportionately populated by people of color and those from lower socio-economic backgrounds. Once incarcerated, individuals often face inhumane conditions, including overcrowding, violence, inadequate healthcare, and lack of access to education and rehabilitation programs. These conditions not only violate basic human rights but also hinder the ability of individuals to reintegrate into society post-release, perpetuating cycles of poverty and recidivism. Moreover, private prisons, driven by profit motives, may have incentives to cut costs at the expense of prisoners' well-being, exacerbating these issues.

Juvenile justice systems exhibit similar disparities, with minority youth being more likely to be tried as adults and receive harsher sentences compared to their white peers. The school-to-prison pipeline illustrates how disciplinary policies in schools disproportionately affect students of color, pushing them out of the educational system and into the criminal justice system. These policies often criminalize minor infractions and rely heavily on law enforcement to handle disciplinary matters that could be addressed through supportive and rehabilitative approaches. The long-term impact on these youth include disrupted education, limited future employment opportunities, and increased likelihood of subsequent involvement with the criminal justice system.

Gender biases within the justice system also contribute to inequities, particularly affecting women and LGBTQ+ individuals. Women, especially those from marginalized backgrounds, often face unique challenges, including higher rates of sexual violence and harassment within the prison system. Gender-specific issues, such as pregnancy and childcare, are frequently neglected, leading to further trauma and disadvantage. LGBTQ+ individuals are at greater risk of violence and discrimination within the legal system, both from law enforcement and within correctional facilities, where they may be placed in unsafe environments due to their gender identity or sexual orientation.

Reform efforts aimed at addressing these inequities must be multi-faceted and systemic. Improving access to quality legal representation for all individuals, regardless of their socio-economic status, is essential. This could involve increasing funding for public defender programs, providing additional resources and training for attorneys who represent marginalized communities, and implementing policies that reduce the reliance on cash bail, which disproportionately affects low-income individuals. Additionally, efforts to address racial and ethnic biases in law enforcement and the broader justice system are crucial. This includes comprehensive training on implicit bias, community policing initiatives, and policies that promote accountability and transparency within police departments.

Judicial reforms should also focus on increasing diversity within the judiciary and promoting sentencing practices that consider the broader context of individuals' lives, including socio-economic factors and the potential for rehabilitation. Expanding the use of restorative justice practices, which focus on repairing harm and reintegrating individuals into the community, can provide more equitable and effective alternatives to traditional punitive measures. Moreover, addressing the conditions within prisons and promoting programs that support education, mental health, and job training can help reduce recidivism and support successful reintegration into society.

The inequities in the justice system are deeply entrenched and multifaceted, requiring sustained and comprehensive efforts to address. By recognizing and challenging the systemic biases that create the illusion of fairness, society can work towards a more equitable and just legal system that truly upholds the principles of justice for all. This involves not only policy changes and institutional reforms but also a broader cultural shift that acknowledges and addresses the root causes of inequality and discrimination within the justice system.

165

Chapter 37: The Misuse of Science

The misuse of science is a pervasive issue that threatens the integrity of scientific inquiry and undermines public trust in scientific findings. When data gets distorted, whether through intentional manipulation or unintentional biases, the consequences can be far-reaching, impacting public policy, healthcare, environmental protection, and many other areas of society. Understanding the mechanisms through which scientific data can be misused and the implications of such misuse is crucial for safeguarding the credibility of science and ensuring that it serves the public good.

One of the primary ways in which science can be misused is through the selective reporting of data. This practice, often referred to as "cherry-picking," involves selectively presenting data that supports a particular hypothesis or agenda while ignoring data that contradicts it. This can occur in various forms, such as highlighting positive results while downplaying or omitting negative ones, or choosing specific data points that paint a favorable picture while disregarding the broader context. Cherry-picking can lead to skewed interpretations of scientific findings and can significantly distort the overall understanding of a research topic.

The pressure to publish, often referred to as "publish or perish," is another factor that can contribute to the misuse of science. In the highly competitive world of academia, researchers are often evaluated based on the quantity and impact of their publications. This pressure can incentivize researchers to engage in questionable practices, such as p-hacking or data dredging, to produce statistically significant results. P-hacking involves manipulating data analysis until statistically significant results are obtained, often through repeated testing or selective inclusion of variables. This practice can result in findings that are not truly reflective of underlying phenomena but are instead artifacts of the data manipulation process.

Funding sources and conflicts of interest also play a significant role in the misuse of science. Research funded by organizations with vested interests in specific outcomes can be biased, either consciously or unconsciously, towards those outcomes. For instance, studies sponsored by pharmaceutical companies may be more likely to report favorable results for their products, while studies funded by the tobacco industry have historically downplayed the health risks associated with smoking. Conflicts of interest can compromise the objectivity of researchers and lead to the distortion of scientific data to align with the interests of funders.

Statistical misinterpretation is another common way in which scientific data can be misused. Statistics are a powerful tool for analyzing data, but they can also be easily manipulated or misunderstood. Misuse can occur through the presentation of relative risks without context, the use of inappropriate statistical tests, or the failure to account for confounding variables. For example, presenting a treatment as reducing the risk of a disease by 50% without stating that the absolute risk reduction is from 2% to 1% can be misleading. Such misrepresentations can lead to public misconceptions about the effectiveness or safety of interventions.

Publication bias, where positive results are more likely to be published than negative or null results, further distorts the scientific literature. This bias creates a skewed perception of reality, as the published studies may not accurately represent the true distribution of findings. Meta-analyses and systematic reviews, which rely on the aggregation of published studies, can be particularly affected by publication bias, leading to overestimations of effect sizes and underestimations of risks or side effects.

The misuse of science is not limited to academic settings; it also extends to public policy and regulatory decisions. Policymakers often rely on scientific evidence to inform decisions on public health, environmental protection, and technological regulation. When scientific data is distorted, it can lead to misguided policies that fail to address, or even exacerbate, societal issues. For example, the distortion of climate science by certain interest groups has delayed critical actions needed to mitigate climate change, resulting in significant environmental and economic consequences.

Media representation of scientific findings can also contribute to the misuse of science. The media plays a crucial role in disseminating scientific information to the public, but it can sometimes sensationalize or oversimplify findings to attract attention. Headlines that exaggerate the implications of a single study or fail to provide context can mislead the public and create false perceptions about the state of scientific knowledge. Moreover, the tendency to focus on controversial or groundbreaking findings can overshadow the gradual and cumulative nature of scientific progress, leading to a distorted view of how science advances.

Misinformation and disinformation in the digital age pose additional challenges to the integrity of science. The rapid spread of information through social media and other online platforms can amplify distorted or false scientific claims, reaching large audiences before they can be effectively debunked. The algorithms that drive content on these platforms often prioritize engagement, meaning sensational or polarizing content can be more widely disseminated than accurate but less attention-grabbing information. This environment creates fertile ground for the spread of pseudoscience and conspiracy theories, further eroding public trust in legitimate scientific research.

The replication crisis, where many scientific studies fail to be replicated by independent researchers, highlights another dimension of the misuse of science. The inability to reproduce results raises questions about the reliability of published findings and suggests that some results may be the product of methodological flaws or deliberate manipulation. Efforts to address the replication crisis include promoting transparency in research methods, encouraging the preregistration of studies, and fostering a culture that values replication and rigorous testing of scientific claims.

Addressing the misuse of science requires a multifaceted approach involving the scientific community, funding agencies, policymakers, and the public. Promoting a culture of integrity and transparency in research is essential. This includes encouraging open access to data and methods, fostering collaboration and peer review, and providing education and training on ethical research practices. Funding agencies can play a role by supporting initiatives that prioritize reproducibility and transparency and by mitigating conflicts of interest through independent oversight.

Policymakers and regulatory bodies must critically evaluate scientific evidence and consider the potential biases and limitations of studies used to inform decisions. Engaging with independent experts and promoting transparent decision-making processes can help ensure that policies are based on robust and unbiased scientific evidence. Additionally, supporting independent research institutions and funding mechanisms that are insulated from commercial interests can help reduce the influence of vested interests on scientific outcomes.

The media has a responsibility to accurately report scientific findings and provide context to help the public understand the nuances of scientific research. Journalists should be trained in science communication and ethics to avoid sensationalism and misrepresentation. Collaborating with scientists and relying on credible sources can enhance the quality of science reporting and help bridge the gap between complex scientific concepts and public understanding.

Public education and scientific literacy are crucial for empowering individuals to critically evaluate scientific information and recognize potential biases and distortions. Promoting science education from an early age and providing resources for lifelong learning can help create an informed citizenry that values and understands the scientific process. Public engagement initiatives, such as science festivals, citizen science projects, and open dialogues between scientists and the community, can also foster a deeper appreciation for science and its role in society.

Chapter 38: Mental Health Stigma

Mental health stigma represents a significant barrier to seeking help, profoundly impacting individuals' lives and the broader societal understanding of mental health. This stigma manifests in various forms, including public stigma, self-stigma, and institutional stigma, each contributing to the reluctance of individuals to seek necessary care. Addressing mental health stigma requires a comprehensive understanding of its origins, manifestations, and consequences, as well as targeted strategies to combat it.

Public stigma refers to the negative stereotypes and prejudices held by society about people with mental health conditions. These stereotypes often portray individuals with mental illnesses as dangerous, unpredictable, weak, or incompetent. Such depictions can be found in media representations, cultural narratives, and everyday conversations, reinforcing misconceptions and fostering fear and discrimination. For instance, movies and television shows frequently depict individuals with mental health conditions as violent criminals or as incapable of leading productive lives. These portrayals not only misrepresent the reality of mental health conditions but also contribute to the societal fear and misunderstanding that drive public stigma.

Self-stigma occurs when individuals internalize these public stereotypes and prejudices, leading to diminished self-esteem and self-worth. When people with mental health conditions believe the negative messages they receive from society, they may feel ashamed, embarrassed, or unworthy of help. This internalized stigma can severely impact their willingness to seek treatment, as they may fear judgment or believe that they do not deserve support. The process of self-stigmatization can create a vicious cycle, where the reluctance to seek help exacerbates the mental health condition, reinforcing feelings of inadequacy and hopelessness.

Institutional stigma involves policies and practices within organizations and systems that limit opportunities and resources for people with mental health conditions. This form of stigma can be seen in healthcare, education, employment, and the legal system. For example, health insurance policies may provide limited coverage for mental health services compared to physical health services, making it financially challenging for individuals to access the care they need. In the workplace, discriminatory hiring practices and a lack of accommodations can prevent individuals with mental health conditions from securing and maintaining employment. Institutional stigma reinforces the barriers to seeking help by making it more difficult for individuals to find and afford appropriate mental health services.

The origins of mental health stigma are complex and multifaceted, rooted in historical, cultural, and social factors. Historically, mental health conditions were often misunderstood and attributed to supernatural forces, moral failings, or character flaws. This lack of understanding led to fear, exclusion, and harsh treatments for those with mental illnesses. As scientific knowledge about mental health has evolved, these outdated beliefs have persisted in various forms, perpetuating stigma. Cultural factors also play a significant role, as different societies have varying beliefs and attitudes about mental health. In some cultures, mental health conditions may be seen as a sign of weakness or as something to be hidden, further stigmatizing individuals and discouraging them from seeking help.

The consequences of mental health stigma are far-reaching and profound, affecting not only individuals with mental health conditions but also their families, communities, and society as a whole. One of the most immediate impacts is the delay or avoidance of seeking treatment. Studies have shown that stigma is a significant barrier to accessing mental health services, with many individuals choosing to suffer in silence rather than face potential judgment or discrimination. This delay in seeking help can lead to the worsening of symptoms, reduced quality of life, and increased risk of chronic conditions, disability, and even suicide.

For families and communities, the stigma surrounding mental health can create an environment of silence and isolation. Families may feel ashamed or embarrassed about a loved one's mental health condition, leading to a lack of open communication and support. This isolation can prevent individuals from receiving the encouragement and assistance they need to seek treatment. Communities that stigmatize mental health conditions may also lack adequate resources and support systems, making it more challenging for individuals to find help within their local area.

On a societal level, mental health stigma contributes to the underfunding and undervaluing of mental health services. Governments and institutions may allocate fewer resources to mental health care, research, and education compared to physical health, reflecting and reinforcing the stigma. This lack of investment can result in insufficient mental health services, long wait times for treatment, and a shortage of trained mental health professionals. Consequently, the overall mental health of the population may suffer, leading to higher rates of untreated mental health conditions, increased healthcare costs, and reduced productivity and economic growth.

Addressing mental health stigma requires a multifaceted approach that involves education, advocacy, policy changes, and cultural shifts. Education is a critical component, as increasing awareness and understanding of mental health can help dispel myths and reduce fear. Public education campaigns that provide accurate information about mental health conditions, their prevalence, and their treatability can challenge stereotypes and encourage more compassionate attitudes. Integrating mental health education into school curricula can also help young people develop a more informed and empathetic perspective on mental health from an early age.

Advocacy efforts are essential for promoting the rights and needs of individuals with mental health conditions. Mental health advocacy organizations play a crucial role in raising awareness, influencing policy, and providing support to individuals and families affected by mental health conditions. These organizations can work to ensure that mental health is prioritized in public health agendas, that policies are inclusive and equitable, and that individuals with mental health conditions have a voice in decision-making processes.

Policy changes are necessary to address institutional stigma and create a more supportive environment for mental health care. Governments and institutions can implement policies that ensure parity between mental health and physical health services, improve access to mental health care, and provide protections against discrimination. For example, mental health parity laws require insurance companies to cover mental health services at the same level as physical health services, reducing financial barriers to treatment. Employment policies that promote mental health awareness, provide accommodations, and protect against discrimination can help create more inclusive workplaces.

Cultural shifts are perhaps the most challenging but also the most critical aspect of reducing mental health stigma. Changing deeply ingrained attitudes and beliefs requires sustained effort and the involvement of all sectors of society. Media and entertainment industries have a powerful influence on cultural perceptions and can play a significant role in challenging stigma by portraying mental health conditions accurately and sensitively. Prominent figures, such as celebrities, athletes, and public leaders, can also help reduce stigma by sharing their own experiences with mental health and advocating for mental health awareness.

Peer support and empowerment are vital components of reducing self-stigma and encouraging individuals to seek help. Peer support programs, where individuals with lived experience of mental health conditions provide support and guidance to others, can help reduce feelings of isolation and shame. These programs can empower individuals to take an active role in their recovery and provide valuable insights and encouragement. Creating safe spaces for individuals to share their experiences and connect with others who understand can foster a sense of community and acceptance.

In addition to these strategies, research plays a crucial role in understanding and addressing mental health stigma. Continued research on the causes and consequences of stigma, as well as the effectiveness of anti-stigma interventions, is essential for developing evidence-based approaches. Research can also help identify specific populations or contexts where stigma is particularly prevalent and tailor interventions accordingly.

Chapter 39: The Price of Convenience

The concept of instant gratification has become deeply embedded in modern society, largely due to advancements in technology and shifts in consumer behavior. Instant gratification refers to the desire for immediate pleasure or reward without delay. While the convenience of instant access to goods, services, and information offers numerous benefits, it also comes with significant downsides. These downsides affect various aspects of life, including mental health, financial stability, social relationships, and environmental sustainability. Understanding the complexities of instant gratification and its long-term consequences is crucial for making informed choices and fostering a more balanced approach to convenience.

The allure of instant gratification is rooted in human psychology. Our brains are wired to seek pleasure and avoid pain, a mechanism that has evolved to ensure survival. Immediate rewards trigger the release of dopamine, a neurotransmitter associated with pleasure and reward. This dopamine rush reinforces the behavior that led to the reward, creating a cycle of craving and seeking immediate satisfaction. In the context of modern life, this means that the availability of instant rewards—whether through online shopping, fast food, social media likes, or on-demand entertainment—can lead to habitual seeking of immediate pleasure, often at the expense of long-term well-being.

One of the most prominent areas affected by the pursuit of instant gratification is mental health. The constant accessibility of stimuli designed to provide quick rewards can lead to various psychological issues. For instance, the overuse of social media platforms, which are engineered to maximize user engagement through likes, comments, and shares, can contribute to anxiety, depression, and low self-esteem. Studies have shown that the frequent checking of social media can create a cycle of seeking validation and experiencing disappointment when the expected social reinforcement is not received. This can lead to a reliance on external validation for self-worth, undermining mental health and resilience.

The pursuit of instant gratification can also impair cognitive functioning and productivity. The constant availability of distractions—such as notifications from smartphones, instant messaging, and streaming services—can fragment attention and reduce the ability to focus on tasks that require sustained effort and concentration. This phenomenon, often referred to as "attention residue," occurs when part of the mind remains focused on a previous task or distraction, reducing the cognitive resources available for the current task. Over time, this can diminish the capacity for deep work, critical thinking, and creative problem-solving, essential skills in both professional and personal contexts.

Financial stability is another area significantly impacted by the culture of instant gratification. The ease of online shopping and the prevalence of credit facilities have made it easier than ever to make impulsive purchases without considering long-term financial implications. This can lead to increased debt and financial stress. For example, buy-now-pay-later schemes and credit card purchases allow consumers to obtain goods immediately while deferring payment, often leading to overspending and the accumulation of high-interest debt. The immediate pleasure of acquiring new items can overshadow the future burden of financial obligations, creating a cycle of spending that is difficult to break.

The environment also bears the brunt of the convenience associated with instant gratification. The demand for fast and convenient products has led to the proliferation of disposable goods, excessive packaging, and fast fashion. These practices contribute significantly to environmental degradation through increased waste, resource depletion, and pollution. For instance, the fast fashion industry, which thrives on quickly producing inexpensive clothing to meet the latest trends, results in enormous amounts of textile waste and environmental pollution from manufacturing processes. Similarly, the convenience of single-use plastics for packaging and disposable products contributes to the growing problem of plastic pollution in oceans and landfills.

Social relationships can be strained by the pursuit of instant gratification as well. The preference for immediate rewards can translate into impatience and a lack of tolerance for delays or inconveniences in interpersonal interactions. This can manifest as a reluctance to invest time and effort into building and maintaining meaningful relationships, which often require patience, compromise, and long-term commitment. For example, the ease of swiping on dating apps for instant connections can create a paradox of choice, where individuals continuously seek the next best option instead of fostering deeper connections with potential partners. This can lead to superficial relationships and a sense of loneliness and dissatisfaction.

The education system is not immune to the effects of instant gratification either. The availability of information at the touch of a button has transformed how students learn and engage with educational material. While technology has made learning more accessible, it has also introduced challenges related to attention spans and information retention. Students accustomed to instant answers may struggle with the patience and perseverance required for in-depth study and critical analysis. The expectation of quick results can undermine the development of essential skills such as research, problem-solving, and the ability to engage in sustained intellectual effort.

Workplace dynamics are also influenced by the culture of instant gratification. Employees may expect immediate feedback and rapid career advancement, sometimes leading to dissatisfaction and disengagement when these expectations are not met. The pressure to respond instantly to emails and messages can create a sense of urgency and stress, disrupting work-life balance and contributing to burnout.

Organizations that prioritize short-term results over long-term strategies may foster an environment where quick fixes are valued over sustainable solutions, potentially undermining overall success and employee well-being.

Addressing the downsides of instant gratification requires a multifaceted approach that involves individual behavior changes, societal shifts, and policy interventions. On an individual level, fostering self-discipline and mindfulness can help manage the impulse for immediate rewards. Techniques such as setting long-term goals, practicing delayed gratification, and developing coping strategies for managing cravings can improve self-control and resilience. For example, creating a budget and sticking to it can help manage financial impulses, while setting designated times for checking social media can reduce its impact on mental health and productivity.

Societal shifts are also necessary to counteract the pervasive culture of instant gratification. Education systems can play a crucial role by emphasizing the importance of patience, perseverance, and long-term planning. Incorporating lessons on financial literacy, environmental sustainability, and mental health awareness into school curricula can equip young people with the skills and knowledge to make informed decisions and resist the lure of immediate rewards. Media literacy education can help individuals critically evaluate the messages they receive from advertising and social media, reducing the impact of external influences on their behavior.

Policy interventions can support these efforts by creating environments that encourage long-term thinking and responsible behavior. Governments and regulatory bodies can implement measures to curb the negative effects of consumerism, such as enforcing stricter regulations on advertising, particularly those targeting vulnerable populations like children and adolescents. Policies that promote sustainable practices, such as reducing plastic waste and encouraging recycling, can help mitigate the environmental impact of convenience.

Additionally, financial regulations that protect consumers from predatory lending practices and encourage responsible borrowing can help address the issue of impulsive spending and debt accumulation.

Technology companies also have a role to play in mitigating the downsides of instant gratification. Designing products and services that prioritize user well-being over engagement metrics can help reduce the negative impact of constant connectivity and instant access. For example, social media platforms can implement features that encourage mindful use, such as reminders to take breaks or tools to monitor and limit screen time. E-commerce platforms can promote sustainable consumption by highlighting eco-friendly products and encouraging thoughtful purchasing decisions.

Community initiatives and support networks can also be effective in addressing the downsides of instant gratification. Peer support groups, counseling services, and community education programs can provide individuals with the resources and encouragement they need to make healthier choices. Creating spaces for community engagement and connection can help counteract the isolation and superficiality associated with the culture of instant gratification, fostering a sense of belonging and mutual support.

Chapter 40: Conclusion

The path to enlightened social change is a multifaceted journey that involves a profound transformation in the way individuals, communities, and societies think and act. This transformation is essential for addressing the complex and interconnected challenges facing the world today, such as inequality, environmental degradation, political instability, and social injustice. Enlightened social change requires a holistic approach that integrates ethical principles, inclusivity, sustainability, and a commitment to continuous learning and adaptation.

Enlightened social change begins with a deep understanding of the issues at hand. This understanding must be informed by accurate, comprehensive data and a willingness to engage with diverse perspectives. Too often, social change efforts falter because they are based on incomplete or biased information. To avoid this pitfall, it is essential to prioritize research and evidence-based decision-making. This involves not only collecting and analyzing data but also ensuring that the data is representative of all segments of society, particularly marginalized and vulnerable groups. By grounding social change efforts in a robust understanding of the issues, we can develop more effective and equitable solutions.

At the heart of enlightened social change is the principle of inclusivity. True progress cannot be achieved unless all members of society are included in the process and benefit from the outcomes. This means actively seeking out and valuing the contributions of people from diverse backgrounds and experiences. It also means addressing systemic barriers that prevent certain groups from participating fully in social, economic, and political life. Inclusivity requires a commitment to equity, which goes beyond equality to recognize and address the specific needs and challenges faced by different groups. For example, policies aimed at reducing poverty must consider the unique barriers faced by women, racial and ethnic minorities, people with disabilities, and other marginalized groups.

Another fundamental aspect of enlightened social change is sustainability. Short-term fixes and superficial solutions are insufficient to address the deep-rooted problems facing society. Sustainable social change requires a long-term perspective and a focus on creating systems and structures that are resilient and adaptable. This involves not only protecting and restoring the natural environment but also ensuring that social and economic systems are equitable and just. Sustainable development must balance the needs of the present with the needs of future generations, ensuring that progress does not come at the expense of the planet or the well-being of future populations.

Education and continuous learning are critical components of the path to enlightened social change. Education empowers individuals with the knowledge and skills they need to participate effectively in society and to advocate for their rights and the rights of others. It also fosters critical thinking, creativity, and a sense of responsibility towards the broader community. Lifelong learning, in particular, is essential in a rapidly changing world where new challenges and opportunities are constantly emerging. By promoting a culture of continuous learning, we can ensure that individuals and communities are better equipped to adapt to change and to drive progress.

Collaboration and partnership are also key to achieving enlightened social change. No single individual, organization, or sector can address the complex challenges facing society on their own. Effective social change requires the collective effort of governments, businesses, civil society organizations, and communities. This means building bridges across different sectors and fostering a spirit of collaboration and mutual support. Partnerships can amplify the impact of individual efforts, leverage diverse resources and expertise, and create synergies that drive innovation and progress.

Ethical leadership is another crucial element of the path to enlightened social change. Leaders at all levels of society have a responsibility to act with integrity, transparency, and accountability. Ethical leadership involves making decisions that are in the best interest of the broader community and the planet, rather than serving narrow self-interests. It also means being willing to listen to and learn from others, to admit mistakes, and to take corrective action when necessary. By setting a positive example and fostering a culture of ethical behavior, leaders can inspire others to follow suit and contribute to a more just and equitable society.

The role of technology in social change cannot be overlooked. Technological advancements have the potential to drive significant progress, but they also present new challenges and risks. On the one hand, technology can enhance communication, improve access to information and services, and facilitate innovative solutions to social problems. On the other hand, it can exacerbate inequalities, infringe on privacy, and create new forms of exploitation and harm. To harness the positive potential of technology while mitigating its risks, it is essential to approach technological development and deployment with a clear ethical framework and a commitment to inclusivity and justice.

Grassroots movements and community engagement are vital to the success of enlightened social change. Change that is driven from the ground up is often more sustainable and effective because it is rooted in the lived experiences and needs of the people it aims to serve. Grassroots movements can mobilize communities, raise awareness, and advocate for policy changes that reflect the interests and aspirations of marginalized and vulnerable groups. Community engagement, in turn, ensures that social change efforts are responsive to local contexts and that they empower individuals and communities to take an active role in shaping their own futures.

Resilience and adaptability are essential qualities for navigating the path to enlightened social change. The challenges facing society are complex and constantly evolving, requiring a flexible and adaptive approach. This means being open to new ideas and perspectives, learning from failures and setbacks, and being willing to adjust strategies and approaches as circumstances change. Building resilience also involves strengthening the capacity of individuals and communities to withstand and recover from shocks and stresses, whether they are economic, social, or environmental.

The pursuit of enlightened social change is ultimately about creating a world that is more just, equitable, and sustainable. It requires a deep commitment to the principles of inclusivity, sustainability, and ethical behavior, as well as a willingness to engage in continuous learning and collaboration. By grounding our efforts in a robust understanding of the issues, valuing the contributions of all members of society, and fostering a spirit of partnership and mutual support, we can create lasting and meaningful change. This journey is challenging and complex, but it is also full of potential and promise. By working together and remaining steadfast in our commitment to these principles, we can build a brighter future for all.

The path to enlightened social change also involves addressing the underlying structures and systems that perpetuate inequality and injustice. This means challenging and transforming the power dynamics, policies, and practices that disadvantage certain groups while privileging others. For example, addressing systemic racism requires not only confronting individual prejudices but also dismantling institutional policies and practices that reinforce racial disparities. Similarly, achieving gender equality involves challenging deeply ingrained cultural norms and ensuring that women and girls have equal access to opportunities and resources.

Engaging in enlightened social change also means recognizing and addressing the interconnectedness of different social issues. Problems such as poverty, environmental degradation, health disparities, and educational inequities are often intertwined, and efforts to address one issue can have ripple effects on others. For example, improving access to quality education can have positive impacts on health, economic opportunities, and social mobility. Similarly, addressing climate change can contribute to reducing poverty and promoting social justice by protecting vulnerable communities from environmental hazards. By adopting a holistic and intersectional approach, we can develop more comprehensive and effective solutions that address the root causes of social problems.

Cultural change is another important aspect of the path to enlightened social change. Cultural norms, values, and practices play a significant role in shaping attitudes and behaviors, and changing these cultural elements can be crucial for achieving lasting social change. This involves challenging harmful stereotypes and biases, promoting positive and inclusive narratives, and fostering a culture of empathy, respect, and solidarity. Cultural change can be facilitated through various means, including education, media, arts, and public discourse. By creating a culture that values and respects diversity, promotes social justice, and encourages active participation in social change efforts, we can create a more supportive environment for progress.

The End.